A MANAGER'S GUIDE
TO PERFORMANCE
APPRAISAL

A MANAGER'S GUIDE TO PERFORMANCE APPRAISAL

Pride, Prejudice,
and the Law of
Equal Opportunity

THOMAS H. PATTEN, JR.

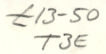

THE FREE PRESS
A Division of Macmillan Publishing Co., Inc.
NEW YORK

Collier Macmillan Publishers
LONDON

The Free Press
A Division of Macmillan Publishing Co., Inc.
866 Third Avenue, New York, N. Y. 10022

Collier Macmillan Canada, Inc.

Library of Congress Catalog Card Number: 82-70540

Printed in the United States of America

printing number
1 2 3 4 5 6 7 8 9 10

Library of Congress Cataloging in Publication Data

Patten, Thomas Henry
    A manager's guide to performance appraisal.

    Bibliography: p.
    Includes index.
    1. Employees, Rating of.   2. Management by objectives.
I. Title.
HF5549.5.R3P37   1982   658.3′125   82-70540
ISBN 0-02-924930-9   AACR2

To my wife Jule, who takes pride in
outstanding performance and
toward whom I am prejudiced

CONTENTS

PREFACE

I HAVE BEEN A STUDENT, user, and recipient of performance appraisal since 1955 when I wrote a master of science thesis on the subject at the New York State School of Industrial and Labor Relations, Cornell University. That credential hardly qualifies me as an expert on the subject because every reader has received "report cards" from school and, as a result, has a personal opinion on what it means to be appraised, as well as thoughts on how the appraisal process could have been improved.

For almost thirty years I have followed what self-proclaimed experts on the subject have written, advocated, implemented, and evaluated. I think I have read at one time or another every major article and book on the subject written in America since World War I, which takes us back, in this field, to the dark ages. In another sense, since opinions about people, their behavior, their strengths, and their weaknesses have been an accompaniment of human society from its beginnings, perhaps no one can assert that he or she has thoroughly researched the subject, which is unresearchable in the broadest sense. To write about performance appraisal is to write about a bucket of steam that is never quite captured in its container. Yet we need not despair. Performance appraisal has become less baffling in recent years, and we know more today about its workings than ever before. There is a need for a book that reduces the bafflement and states clear guidelines for managers who give and receive performance appraisals. For them, I unabashedly endorse MBO (management by objectives) in this book because I think it has more of the answers we seek than any other methods.

Managers need to know what works and to be able to have confidence in a presentation on the subject which crystallizes the best thinking available based upon research, company and agency practice, and existing public policy.

I intend that this book meet this challenging managerial need. Consequently, I have tried to digest as much solid, no-nonsense advice on the subject as possible and to present it clearly and prescriptively, with as few qualifications as absolutely needed. I assume the responsibility for any resulting deficiencies but I hope they are minimal and acceptable if my main purpose of providing sensible assistance to the practicing manager is attained.

ACKNOWLEDGMENTS

Robert Wallace, Senior Editor of The Free Press, encouraged me to write this book in response to a widespread need among managers—a need that seems never to be met despite the outpouring of books and articles on performance appraisal.

My daughter Laurie typed the manuscript, which was a real written-by-hand project completed during a 1981 sabbatical leave from Michigan State University.

My graduate assistant at Michigan State University during 1981–1982, Paul Reagan, read the manuscript, offered criticisms, and helped me through the various revision stages, making many substantive suggestions that I found helpful and used.

I thank everyone named for their help, and I accept all blame for errors of omission and commission—and in some cases simplification when we all knew the issue discussed was much more complex than I cared to admit in a short book.

A MANAGER'S GUIDE TO PERFORMANCE APPRAISAL

1

The search for the Holy Grail in performance appraisal is bound to go on for years.

P ERFORMANCE APPRAISAL has remained an unsolved and perhaps unsolvable problem in human-resource management. The amount of thinking, writing, and debating that surrounds the topic is truly massive.[1] The progress made from the 1920s to the present in devising workable new performance appraisal systems is meager and in a practical sense leads to but one place in the 1980s, the installation and use of management by objectives (MBO) for performance-based pay. To be sure, many gimmicky innovations have been devised for reviewing managerial and employee performance, yet they have proven to be short-lived. The search for the Holy Grail in performance appraisal goes on.

Why hasn't the search been completed after at least sixty years of serious casting about? Is discovery imminent? Should the quest be declared over, and should management settle down to accepting that there is no solution to the problem of appraising (let alone measuring) the performance of people at work?

In this book we take still another look at the subject and try to cut a swath through a field overgrown with repetitive, shallow, and unexciting gimmicks. Our theme is new to the performance review field: the management of human pride and prejudice confounds the search for the most practical method. The sources of pride and prejudice and their interplay are numerous. The interplay can and must be handled effectively.

The manager who "gives" the performance review enters the appraisal interview already hoping the well-prepared list of the employee's successes and shortfalls is accurate and will be accepted gracefully. The manager's pride is on the line, and he[2] will defend it. The manager believes that the prepared review is fair and unprejudiced. If the employee's performance has been borderline or poor, the manager may be apprehensive yet optimistic that rationality will prevail and the employee will not lash back out of anger when told he is not so hot on the job. Yet employees too have their pride to defend, and few want to hear the bad news about what the boss thinks of them. Employees prejudge themselves defensively, especially if they perceive themselves as working under a performance-based pay system and do not want to hear about why their pay increase is going to be small (or withheld).

The personnel manager who has established a particular performance appraisal system in his firm or agency has an investment in that system. His pride is involved in his choice to go with a particular system and, by the same token, he is likely to be prejudiced against systems tried in the past that did not work out or systems used by others that are thought to be inferior to his own.

Put another way, performance appraisal needs to be seen in a matrix of pride and prejudice. To say this is not to use the gimmickry of the past in order to approach the subject from a new angle, only to leave the reader with no real insight.

Performance appraisal is a human process, and it is inevitable in any work organization in the private or public sector. The only basic questions are: (1) will the appraisal be formal or informal, and (2) will the system be accepted and used by managers as intended by the creators of the system? It is *not* possible to decide there will be *no* appraisal system at all. It is *not* reasonable to conclude that managers will create *no* systems on their own. They will have to differentiate between their subordinate employees because individuals differ in how well they do on the job. Rewards must be meted out correspondingly if a work force is to be stabilized and is to become cohesive. In this context, prejudice and pride also take on another—and very contemporary—face. In fact, there is a real danger in allowing managers to devise their own highly personalized, homemade hip-pocket performance review forms or to take other actions that are naive and detrimental to people.

Prejudice is against the law when it is manifested as denial of equal employment opportunity (EEO) and equal pay for equal work. This facet of performance appraisal is relatively new and signifies now that the courts and government agencies are very strongly in the picture.[3] Sexism, ageism, and racism as types of biases must be combatted as a matter of public policy. In a positive sense, the performance review systems can be used for implementing EEO by requiring managers to have as part of their work objective the attainment of specific minority recruitment, training, and promotion goals. Such an approach makes the performance appraisal system a much more visible tool for human resource management and development in the total sense. Organizational pride and embarrassment are thus inextricably tied up with the gloomy public record of employment discrimination and prejudice versus free mobility for people from all spheres of society. Performance review is thus once again in the spotlight and will continue to be scrutinized and used in new ways in the 1980s. In fact, it is more important than ever as an administrative tool for the management of human resources.

The remainder of this book is an examination of forty-five practical guides that are no-nonsense rules of thumb for managers who must "give" performance reviews to subordinates as part of their work. The extent to which the guidelines are affected by the human resource/personnel management department (called HR/PMD for the remainder of the book) is also discussed where needed because both the manager and HR/PMD interface closely in the creation and administration of appraisal systems.

It is sometimes futile to urge managers to conduct themselves in desirable ways when the monitors of the personnel systems and policies with which they must work behave in ways that make desirable managerial approaches impossible. Thus, while we have managers always in mind, we sometimes leave them temporarily to examine the constraints imposed on them by their company or agency. Then we return to the home ground of the manager and spell out the implications of the slight tangent for the manager, thereby rounding out the picture.

2

Measure or appraise performance as behavior; forget about personality traits.

W E ARE INTERESTED PRIMARILY in how employees carry out their assigned tasks and work. We use performance appraisal as a tool for this purpose: to assist in delegating the carrying out of work and to control the conduct of the work so that the planned results are obtained. Performance appraisal can therefore be regarded as an administrative tool for planning and controlling the assignment of work and how well or poorly it is completed.

Once one grasps this basic conception of performance appraisal, it becomes easy to see why the proper focus in an appraisal is upon what an employee does, not upon amateur psychoanalysis about the traits that "explain" the good and bad results, apparent and observable. Performance is always in the eye of the beholder and the performing employee. The trick is for both the boss and the subordinate to avoid prejudicial views and to examine behavior.

It might seem strange to advocate a focus upon behavior

when the manager is asked to rate his subordinates according to a so-called graphic rating scale. Figure 2.1 displays such a scale. Performance appraisal (or merit rating as it was termed fifty and sixty years ago) was started at a time (the 1920s) when "trait psychology" was in its heyday. Consequently, many of the systems of performance review that persist today are based upon a psychological theory that has long since been discredited as overly simplistic, naive, and conceptually inadequate. The human individual is not best understood as a creature composed of various amounts of initiative, cooperativeness, loyalty, perseverance, or the like. These terms may be useful for communicating in a compressed way about how a particular person's behavior pattern appears and allow for comparisons and contrasts with some other employee's typical behavior pattern. But the comparative advantages of trait rating are relatively weak and what few there are crumble in the hands of a manager who does not use the English language rigorously or who poorly observes and "rates" employees at work. A humorous example of the problem is seen is Figure 2.2.

To sit down with an employee and discuss with him (the ratee) what you (the rater) think of his "traits" (especially if the ratee's job results are meager or inadequate) invites controversy and clashes that can be most unnerving and damaging. Worse, such encounters can polarize rater-ratee relations and create durable animosities that are never settled—until one or the other is transferred or quits! These difficulties can be avoided if we steer clear of trait names.

In view of their serious drawbacks, it is nevertheless surprising that graphic rating scales are in widespread use. First, they are easy to construct, easy to score, and applicable to a variety of jobs. Second, they take less time to complete than more complex forms and filling them out requires less thought. Third, they have been around for years; and some managers feel very comfortable with them, especially if employees never see the forms and the forms are merely sent to the personnel

FIGURE 2.1 Example of a Graphic Rating Scale with Trait Names

(Name of School)

Employer's Evaluation of Cooperative Student

Name _____ Class _____ Course _____

Work Period _____ Assignment _____

Employer _____

INSTRUCTIONS: The immediate supervisor will evaluate the student objectively, comparing him with other students of comparable academic level, with other personnel assigned the same or similarly classified jobs, or with individual standards.

RELATIONS WITH OTHERS
- ☐ Exceptionally well accepted
- ☐ Works well with others
- ☐ Gets along satisfactorily
- ☐ Has some difficulty working with others
- ☐ Works very poorly with others

ATTITUDE – APPLICATION TO WORK
- ☐ Outstanding in enthusiasm
- ☐ Very interested and industrious
- ☐ Average in diligence and interest
- ☐ Somewhat indifferent
- ☐ Definitely not interested

JUDGMENT
- ☐ Exceptionally mature
- ☐ Above average in making decisions
- ☐ Usually makes the right decision
- ☐ Often uses poor judgment
- ☐ Consistently uses bad judgment

DEPENDABILITY
- ☐ Completely dependable
- ☐ Above average in dependability
- ☐ Usually dependable
- ☐ Sometimes neglectful or careless
- ☐ Unreliable

ABILITY TO LEARN
- ☐ Learns very quickly
- ☐ Learns readily
- ☐ Average in learning
- ☐ Rather slow to learn
- ☐ Very slow to learn

QUALITY OF WORK
- ☐ Excellent
- ☐ Very good
- ☐ Average
- ☐ Below average
- ☐ Very poor

ATTENDANCE
- ☐ Regular   ☐ Irregular

PUNCTUALITY
- ☐ Regular   ☐ Irregular

OVERALL PERFORMANCE:

Outstanding	Very Good	+ Average –	Marginal	Unsatisfactory

What traits may help or hinder the student's advancement?

_____

Additional Remarks (over if necessary):

_____

This report has been discussed with student   ☐ Yes   ☐ No

(Signed) _____   Date _____
(Immediate Supervisor)

This form is recommended by the Cooperative Education Division, ASEE

Sources: Thomas H. Patten, Jr., *Manpower Planning and the Development of Human Resources* (New York: Wiley, 1971), p. 510 and Thomas H. Patten, Jr., *Pay, Employee Compensation and Incentive Plans* (New York: Free Press, 1977), p. 354.

FIGURE 2.2 Sample Comments from Military Officer Efficiency Reports

This officer has talents but has kept them well hidden.
Combs his hair to one side and appears rustic.
A quiet, reticent, neat-appearing officer--industrious, tenacious, diffident, careful, and neat. I do not wish to have this officer as a member of my command at any time.

Does not drink but is a good mixer.
Can express a sentence in two paragraphs at a time.
His leadership is outstanding except for his lack of ability to get along with his subordinates.
He has failed to demonstrate any outstanding weaknesses.

He hasn't any mental traits.
His departure is in no way considered a loss. In fact, it is a gain. His transfer was concurred in by all commanders with relief.
He needs careful watching since he borders on the brilliant.
A particularly fine appearance when astride a horse.

Believes sincerely in the power of prayer and it is astonishing to note how many times his prayers are answered.
A tall, stocky officer.
Open to suggestions but never follows same.
Never makes the same mistake twice but it seems to me that he has made them all once.

He has begun to fraternize without realizing it.
In any change of policy or procedure, he can be depended upon to produce the improbable hypothetical situation in which the new policy will not work.
Gives the appearance of being fat due to the tight clothes he wears.
Is keenly analytical, and his highly developed mentality could best be used in the research and development field. He lacks common sense.

He has developed into a good all round staff officer.
Tends to overestimate himself and underestimate the problem, being surprised and confused by the resulting situations.
An independent thinker with a mediocre mentality.
Maintains good relations unilaterally.

Recently married and devotes more time to this activity than to his current assignment.
An exceptionally well qualified officer with a broad base.
Tends to create the impression of unpositive personality through needless and undiscerning gentility and soft-spokenness.
Of average intelligence except for lack of judgment on one occasion in attempting to capture a rattlesnake for which he was hospitalized.

Source: Unknown. Reproduced from Thomas H. Patten, Jr., *Pay: Employee Compensation and Incentive Plans* (New York: Free Press, 1977), p. 357.

office where they are used as merit rating for the purpose of determining the amount of a merit (pay) increase that should be granted an employee.

Unfortunately, in the contemporary environment in America, almost all of the alleged advantages of graphic rating scales can lead into legal controversy. Many states have privacy laws that allow employees to see which company and agency records are retained as official employment documents. Information so discovered can be controverted by an employee, and cases may be made that appraisals were biased and are unsupported by the real facts of job performance. Thus, the handy-dandy graphic rating scale is probably heading toward the personnel scrap heap during the 1980s—on legal as well as psychological grounds.

The use of graphic rating scales in the near term may be justifiable in one way, particularly if the manager using them can buttress the trait-name evaluation with relevant job facts. Managers who have responsibility for a large number of clerical workers, secretaries, and technicians, who are essentially subordinates with stable and repetitive jobs, may find that they can give a meaningful and successful performance appraisal by using a graphic rating scale, up-to-date job description, and list of observed on-the-job accomplishments. Such managers may resist extensive record-keeping and goal-setting sessions with clerical, office, and technical subordinates on the grounds that they lack the time for such low payoff busy work. Managers will fill out graphic rating scales—in fact they prefer to do them, particularly if they are either extremely busy or extremely lazy!

This willingness to comply by filling in forms in no way obviates any of the potential legal problems stemming from accusations of prejudice in the administration of the review. But it does suggest a limited place for the possible application of graphic rating scales in the current human-resource scene. Yet it should be regarded as a dangerous place—and one that could prove very hard to defend in court. In fact, the courts have consistently held that graphic rating scales allow uncontrolled bias to enter performance appraisal judgments.

It should be obvious from what has been discussed above that it is better to measure or appraise performance as behavior rather than using trait names. Several caveats are in order. Measurement in the strict sense is virtually impossible for many jobs—or is applicable only in gross and misleading ways for the trivial aspects of the work, such as the number of mailable letters that an executive secretary types daily. Even in industrial engineering, most work measurement methods do not attempt to measure the work content directly but instead count the time required to complete a certain number of units, such as fifty widgets per hour. Put another way, the measurement of performance consists of comparing actual results with production standards (the planned results). Moreover, much managerial and professional work admits of few meaningful ''measurement'' possibilities, although it does offer grounds for ''review'' or ''appraisal'' that reduce subjectivity to a very low level. There is considerable evidence that output measures do provide reliable criteria, and they should be used wherever possible.

Succinctly put, performance appraisal is a formal method of evaluating employees that assumes that employee performance can be observed and assessed although often it cannot be objectively measured by units produced in elapsed time. Some managers observe better than others and, consequently, appraise employees more adequately than others. Managers who appraise more adequately focus upon behavior exhibited by employees. Such managers are not necessarily invigilators who intrude into employees' life space at work and become microscopic in their observation. Rather they are clear on what is expected of the employee in job results, and by perusing work turned in, reports, participation in meetings, body language, and all the other signs and symbols that pass their eyes, they draw inferences about performance. The focus is on observable behavior, not traits.

To urge that all managers should focus upon behavior is not in any sense to underestimate the difficulties some people have in learning how to be adequate, if not astute, observers. To some extent, observational skills can be improved with training. Yet it would be unrealistic to expect that every industrial or public-sector manager will develop the acuity of a social anthropologist who is sent off to study and record Pacific Islanders and their way of life.

In general, it is much easier to communicate the appraised performance and to get a handle on exactly what it is we are talking about when we speak about observed behavior. To be sure, there may be important differences in perceptions and behavioral inferences discussed by the observer and the observed. These differences can, however, be narrowed down and pinpointed so that the discussion becomes constructive and clearer than is the case when trait names are tangled up by a semantically snarled pair of people.

Although every work organization, whether it wants to or not or realizes it or not, ends up appraising employees, many companies and agencies have no formal appraisal program. Perhaps only about one-half of the large organizations in America have them for salaried employees and virtually none of the millions of tiny businesses has any type of formal appraisal system. Organizations that do have programs are likely to have several types of subprograms of appraisal that cater to specific employee groups. For example, unionized firms may have no formal programs for factory production and maintenance employees because the union objects to performance appraisal. In these cases, management may measure employee performance by reference to formal work standards and, through the use of disciplinary procedures, may enforce the rules pertaining to acceptable levels of production. Or management may maintain an individual, group, or plant-wide productivity plan to encourage performance. The union would probably prefer that all personnel transactions affecting its members be based strictly on seniority and couldn't care less about the quality of performances unless pressed to the wall in the case of a plant shutdown or agency closure.

Clerical employees and technicians usually perform work that can be appraised most easily, although some aspects of it can often be measured—and properly measured. For example, in some routinized clerical jobs, an actual measure of files maintained, telephone calls handled, supervisors serviced, deadlines for mailings met, and the like, can help in evaluating performance although some of the less concrete aspects of the work may need to be appraised. The latter might include: courtesy, cooperation with employees in other departments, and maintaining the confidentiality of files.

Professional, managerial, and top executive employees perform work that is best appraised and seldom measured in an industrial-engineering sense. To be sure, some of the measures of enterprise success may appropriately be applied to the performance of executives who fill major line and staff positions. These include such measures as: profit as a percentage of sales, percentage of return on investment, performance against budget, and numerous other financial indices. But in a broader sense, much of what professional employees, managers, and top executives do is best appraised, which implies some subjective, judgmental aspects, provided they are anchored clearly in job content.

3

Concentrate on a critique of work done, not on the mystique or potential for work yet to be done.

THEORETICALLY, APPRAISALS could focus upon the past, present, and future behavior of employees. In practice, we need to distinguish between present and past performance and some estimate of an employee's future performance (or potential, as it is commonly termed).

A performance appraisal should be geared to an employee's past behavior, covering the time since his last performance review to the present. Normally, a performance appraisal should be given annually with the exception of employees in a probationary status; these employees should be given reviews at intervals of three and six months and annually thereafter.

A common practice is to provide performance reviews on the annual anniversary of the employee's first day of employment. But this is merely an administrative convenience. Any date during the year is acceptable, and some managers find that "bunching" the reviews together at a certain time of the year for all their subordinates is convenient and provides a chance to concentrate simultaneously on a set of relative performances. Managers feel that such a procedure may enhance the validity of the ratings. Provided they do not rush through the bunched appraisals, the end of the year review may be a good idea.

It matters little how often probationary employees are given reviews as long as the quality of their performance is made known to them before a full year elapses. Ninety-day and six-month reviews are merely conventional.

Insofar as performance reviews should focus on present and immediate past behavior, there is no reason why a performance appraisal cannot be given at any time when in the judgment of the manager there would be value in so doing. For example, if an employee's performance has deteriorated or improved dramatically, a manager would be wise to draw up and administer a performance review in recognition of the changed behavior. In this way the true value of a performance review is manifest. It is a managerial tool to be used for improving results under the manager's province. But it should not be used punitively and unjustly. Nowadays, an employee who feels that the appraisal has been used as a lash by a prejudiced manager may sue the employer in an effort to seek fair treatment. Of course, management cannot run the business properly if it is in constant fear of the law and the costly, prolonged, debilitating defenses that accompany a lawsuit. Yet it should not hesitate to exercise its prerogative to manage the work force. The performance appraisal is a legitimate device for securing adequate on-the-job behavior and should be used to do so.

These matters bring us to the question of how much of the past behavior of an employee is relevant for inclusion in the performance review? The answer is, "All of it," although the performance review is never intended to be a total summary of what an employee has done in the past without regard to how long ago the performance took place. The objective is to state fairly and accurately the *typical* behavior of an employee in the period covered by the review. This is a difficult task; it is difficult to paint Rembrandts if one is not Rembrandt. Yet the manager must strive to portray the employee's performance in a way that somehow captures what was actually observed. Accent should be on the typical, which may create a problem in differences of perception between the rater and ratee, manager and employee. Managers, however, by virtue of their position, are obliged to report what they perceive as typical. It is important that they should not focus on the *atypical* and render performance reviews that are unfair, unbalanced, or unsound. In such cases, employees could argue that the performance review was dictated by prejudice and could probably make persuasive *prima facie* cases of unfair treatment from which prejudice can reasonably be inferred.

In summary, performance review takes place in the present looking as far backward as a year. Performances prior to the year in question should not generally have a bearing on the performance appraisal applicable in a given year. It is legitimate for a manager to consult the official company or agency records in preparation for the review of the performance of an employee. Information obtained in this way, however, should be regarded as ancient history and not allowed to have much relevance to the purpose at hand. The record may indicate spectacular swings in performance, consistency, an upward trend, a downward trend, or many other behavioral patterns. They may mean little for the purpose at hand; and certainly rewards or punishments of past years need not be rehashed unless there are extenuating circumstances, new facts, or special connections that need to be made for relating the present and past years. By and large, it is best to disregard ancient history; there is no reason to repunish or re-reward. Start the slate anew.

It may actually be a good idea to purge the files of performance reviews from over five years back—or maybe even three years. Purges may, of course, rid the company or agency of documentation they may need to defend themselves in a complex lawsuit. But companies and agencies should not be run backwards by performance appraisal history; rather, the emphasis should be on the performance appraisal as a dynamic tool of the present, applicable right now to a specific situation and manager-employee set or pair.

As for the future, performance appraisal should be separated from estimates of future potential. It is difficult to predict future performance in an employee's present job and equally tough to estimate his potential for other jobs in the same occupation, different occupations, higher pay grades, and the top management levels (five or ten or more years from the present). Yet it is argued that an employee's organizational superiors are in the best position to make these predictions because they have knowledge of what an employee has attained in the past. And everyone knows: one's past accomplishments are the best predictor of the future!

On the surface, we might consider it is reasonable to assume that a manager should be able to make a fairly shrewd guess as to whether an employee has potential for: (1) management, or (2) continuing nonmanagerial growth as an individual contributor, or (3) both. The manager may also be expected to be able to estimate whether the employee can be moved developmentally in (1) or (2) now, or within two years, or never (in the event that he or she has a health problem or has expressed a desire to retire in the relatively near future). To be sure, a particular manager may be a very shrewd guesser and quite willing to provide the HR/PMD with a private estimate of an employee's potential. But the same manager may be reluctant to share and defend these future potential assessments with employees face to face.

These reasonable assumptions do not place insuperable burdens on many managers but it should be recognized that the estimates amount to crystal-ball gazing. They may be better than nothing. But they are likely to be infinitely inferior to estimates of potential determined by an adequate, professionally administered assessment center. These centers provide insight into employees that range beyond the appraisal of one boss and tap into the multiple judgments of participating managers and professionals in the assessment center. The centers are preferable for these reasons; moreover, the prognostications of one boss may be at variance with the potential estimates of previous bosses, which further suggests the invalidity and unreliability of potential assessments by individual managers.

There is still another problem in tying together past, present, and future performance appraisal. Any future potential appraisal is likely to be written in a way that is consistent with what a manager states on paper about prior performance. Except for older or ill employees, the strong present performers are likely to be perceived as having potential for other attractive developmental jobs or higher-level jobs. Average and weak performers are perceived as either improperly placed or of low potential. These predictions of the future could be surmised from a study of performance appraisals of the present, and the written formulation of them adds little or nothing to the sophistication of an organization's human-resource systems.

4

Keep the system simple, and keep the paperwork burden down.

THE DEATH OF MANY PERFORMANCE APPRAISAL SYSTEMS and the failure of others to be born has been caused by human-resource experts who have created complex, paper-laden systems. Managers recoil at the sight. While one may recognize the desirability of formalizing what always comes into existence informally (namely, the evaluation of people), the price to be paid in time, effort, and energy is too high.

Let us take a closer look at why complexity and excessive paperwork have arisen and what managers can do about it. Basically, the simple graphic rating scales that have dominated the field for years have caused distress for managers who give reviews and ulcers for personnel technicians who devise systemic improvements. The technicians have tried to service managers by coming up with new concepts and techniques for measurement and appraisal. Also, out of a desire for organizational survival, personnel technicians have spent millions on paperwork systems, pretty forms, technicolor training films, elaborate records, lengthy files, and the like in efforts to strengthen this administrative tool.

Only a cynic would dismiss all this activity as a lifelong makework project for the personnel technician. The evolution of performance appraisal systems, to hit the highlights, from graphic rating scales to critical incidents, forced choice,[4] and MBO is a history of a movement from simplicity in concept to complexity and back to simplicity again. This is not the place to recapitulate that history in detail. The minor blips on the radar screen of performance review history, such as the use of the forced distribution of rated employees, field review of appraisals, and BARS (behaviorally anchored rating scales),[5] represent changes in technique that also need not divert our attention from what is preferable, namely, a simple, reasonably reliable, and valid system involving little paperwork and low cost.

The particular approach I advocate and variants on it have been widely used in American industry. The approach is built around MBO and performance standards concepts. It will be sketched here, and I return to it for other purposes later in the book.

The approach adds one new conceptual underpin to performance appraisal. We have already seen appraisal as a tool of performance planning and control. The approach is also based upon the assumption that managers are responsible for the development of subordinates who report directly to them. In taking an interest in the development of their subordinates, managers make their own jobs easier because their people gradually become more proficient in the conduct of assigned work and managers can more confidently and comfortably delegate work.

One of the most efficient ways for managers to develop subordinates is to keep them clearly informed of their responsibilities and of how well they are performing in those areas. Employees whose performances are deficient in one way or another can be given training or coaching to meet the standards set by the organizational superior or agreed upon through MBO goal setting. At the same time, the manager can work closely with subordinates to discuss work assignments and to plan their completion. It would be hoped that the manager can create a trustful interpersonal climate in which self-development is stimulated and interpersonal communication is reasonably open and authentic. Within this climate, a performance appraisal can be used both to control the assignment of work and ensuing results and to develop subordinates.

Any seasoned manager knows that, in using performance appraisals for developing human resources, individual employee development depends only to a minor extent upon the particular form of paperwork used. The major variable affecting employee development is usually the quality of the give and take in the relationship between the manager and the employee. This assumes that individuals learn job responsibilities as they start to identify with and obtain insight into the workings of the business or agency that employs them. Learning, of course, takes time and the acquisition of skill, knowledge, and appropriate attitudes should be reflected in increasing competency on the job. It is by no means incorrect to characterize managers as teachers or learning facilitators in the industrial setting.

Underlying the use of performance appraisals is the day-to-day evaluation of employees by managers. Inasmuch as appraisals are an integral part of the work situation and conduct of job assignments, managers who perform capably are likely to look upon the performance appraisal situation as simply an occasion on which the day-to-day informal appraisals passed on to employees in the medium of daily contact are formalized for the record. To this extent, the particular day on which the formal appraisal is held should contain no surprises. Unfortunately, we often find that the performance appraisal is accompanied by trauma and strife when the manager has failed to communicate his evaluation of the employee's behavior informally in daily contacts.

The simple type of performance review system I have in mind can best be presented by reference to Figure 4.1. The form is very stark. The employee's name and certain basic information on his job and location in the organization are shown. The date of the performance review and the period covered by the appraisal are indicated as well.

The form itself lists the various job duties of the employee on the left-hand side of the page. On the right is a list of the performance incidents or trends that typify the employee's performance since the last appraisal. This type of form is particularly useful because the manager giving the performance review is guided by the boundaries of the job description and need simply list on the left the employee's specific position responsibilities. These duties can be derived either from the goals agreed upon in MBO sessions in which the manager and employee engaged or from the official position description of the employee's assigned work. In the latter case we can pinpoint the performance standards that apply to the employee's work and use them in the performance appraisal.

Considerable freedom is afforded by this form in stating MBO goals, performance standards, and job duties and responsibilities. Naturally, it is possible to use as many sheets of paper as necessary to accommodate specification of the different responsibilities for work content, EEO goal implementation, employee-development goal implementation, the quality of the manager's administrative practices, and other matters deemed worthy of appraisal. Normally, one side of an ordinary 8½ × 11 sheet of paper would be sufficient to list the responsibilities for almost all employees because once the listing includes more than five to eight major duties, the remainder are on a lesser plane of importance.

On the right side of the page, the performance that typifies the employee's performance can be stated and lined up against the specific responsibilities. It is important to emphasize that the performance incidents or trends listed are those that are typical (rather than those that are unusual) and

FIGURE 4.1 Performance Review Form Emphasizing Standards, Objectives, and Employee Behavior on the Job

Name	Soc. Sec. No.	Period from Covered	To	Date of Review
Department	Staff, Division, Branch	Organization Code No.		Classification

Position Responsibilities	Performance Incidents or Trends That Typify Employee's Performance Since Last Review

Improvements or Lack of Improvements Since Last Review

Specific Action To Be Taken To Improve Performance

Are the Normal Requirements Met Regarding:
Attendance Yes   No   Punctuality   Yes ☐ No ☐
If Not, Explain.

Describe Any Other Characteristics Which Affect the Employee's Performance and Which Require Classification.

Prepared by	Title	Reviewed by	Title

Employee's Comments (Freely Express Your Views on the Completeness of the Review, Accuracy, Etc.)

Use back of page if necessary.

Employee's Signature	Date

Sources: Thomas H. Patten, *Manpower Planning and the Development of Human Resources* (New York: Wiley, 1971), p. 271 and Thomas H. Patten, Jr., Pay: *Employee Compensation and Incentive Plans* (New York: Free Press, 1977), p. 374.

adequately characterize the employee's performance since his last review. The recent and the old need to be "averaged" to characterize the typical review. Training may be necessary to help managers know how incidents and trends can be observed, recorded, and inserted on the performance appraisal form, thereby showing them how to avoid some of the possible pitfalls, such as focussing either on an inappropriate time frame or sample of behavior.

On the bottom of Figure 4.1 are several categories of information. Improvements or lack of improvements since the employee's last performance appraisal may be noted. Specific actions to be taken to improve performance, as agreed, also may be listed. These can later be referred to by the manager to formulate employee development plans.

For managers who wish to make observations on the employee's attendance and punctuality, there is a small amount of space to describe any other characteristics that affect the employee's performance and that require clarification. Again, additional pages or space can be used for comments the manager wishes to make relative to the items of information that appear on the bottom of the performance review form.

The last few lines of the appraisal form contain additional descriptive information concerning the manager who prepared the form and the manager's boss who reviewed the prepared appraisal before it was administered. By involving two levels of management in the preparation and administration of the performance appraisal, the manager who conducts the performance review is placed in a stronger position to fulfill his role than he would be had he not discussed the appraisal with his superior. This is not only a strength grounded in multiple judgments and organizational power; it is also likely to be one that controls against prejudicial reviews and fosters the protection of individual dignity and personal pride. Specifically, the manager-rater has had his organizational superior review the form and make any adjustments that the latter considers significant. This imposes a control for consistency in rating standards by subordinate managers who report to him. Thus, the employee-ratee normally will perceive that the review is just and not merely based upon the unchallenged opinion of his immediate superior.

Still another feature of the form is the space allocated for the employee to address himself to the completeness and accuracy of the review or other matters that he thinks were omitted or improperly stated.

Obviously, employees experiencing a performance review are in a situation that involves the exercise of authority and may have their pride, sense of self-worth, and ego bruised. The MBO and performance standards concepts used in modern pace-setting performance appraisals are intended to remove some of the authoritarian sting of the business or agency and inject in its place some democratic participation and self-protection for the employee being appraised. These features are consistent with contemporary concepts in applied behavioral science as to what makes for the effective management of human resources and the proper managerial style for the 1980s. Nevertheless, it would be naive to assume that many employees will disagree with the reviews and feel perfectly free to express their reactions. The opportunity, however, for some employee feedback is provided on the form, and this feedback is likely to be obtained when employees feel sufficiently aggrieved, frustrated, or unintimidated.

Lastly, the employee is asked to sign the review simply to indicate that it was given, not that he necessarily agrees with the manager's appraisal. If the employee refuses to sign, the manager need simply indicate that the former refused to sign. In these situations, some avenue of appeal should be open so that the dissatisfied employee either can obtain an interview with the boss of the manager-rater or perhaps can discuss his own plight with an appropriate individual in the company or agency's personnel department. The appeal procedure is especially important as it encourages the employee to ask for an internal review of the appraisal rather than leaving him with no alternative but to run thoughtlessly to a governmental agency for support. Put another way, organizational due process is preferable to seeking the same via a governmental investigation and/or litigation.

In brief, it is possible to have a workable simple system of performance appraisal rather than one based on expensive trappings and a paper monster. Managers who feel put upon by a complex system have every right to demand a better, simpler one because they are available.

5

Be prepared to have more than one performance appraisal system and to have separate appraisal systems oriented toward pay determination and toward employee development—at least for a while.

M ANAGERS MAY HAVE SUBORDINATES in positions encompassing clerical, office, technical, and supervisory work. We have already seen that business firms and government agencies are likely to sustain several systems that cater to different job families. Managers need to be acquainted with these systems and how to use them for planning and controlling work as well as for developing subordinates. This is a training task that should enable managers to acquire the requisite skills, knowledge, and attitudes.

There is another facet of the idea of having separate systems. It is conventional wisdom among many performance appraisal experts that companies and agencies should establish and maintain two entirely different performance appraisal systems: one geared to making pay decisions and one designed to yield information about employee development. The pay-decision system has its roots in the hoary idea of merit rating for merit increases. The employee-development system has its roots in the post–World War II personnel field and its concern with individual, management, and organization development, reflecting respectively the major topics of 1950s, 1960s, and 1970s in the management of human resources.

Can the twain meet or are they forever disparate? Let us begin with the use of performance appraisals in employee development.

Today, companies and agencies use appraisals primarily for assessing the on-the-job behavior (or alleged "traits") governing how individuals perform work tasks. The appraisal is a lever that is used to improve performance, coach employees on how to do better, or take action regarding people who have reached plateaus or declined in performance. The appraisal, when used in an optimal way, provides a data base for fostering desirable outcomes, which one hopes are of a positive nature but, if not, of at least a constructive nature in the long run. As we have previously remarked, the performance appraisal can be used at any time when it may prove useful to encourage employees or to give them recognition for a job well done. The appraisal thus becomes a supplement to formal on-the-job training and is used to articulate and highlight what the manager perceives in the behavior of subordinates.

Performance appraisal experts have long argued that a tool intended to serve a developmental purpose cannot simultaneously serve a pay-determination purpose. These two purposes are not only best served by different rating systems but are also most effectively utilized when the appraisal for each purpose happens at a different time of the year and, of course, in separate sessions. For the operating manager, this requirement of dual systems means double the work and double the time devoted to the administration of appraisals—a seemingly intolerable and unnecessary burden. What can be done about this?

The answer depends upon the sophistication and stage of development of a company or agency. Small and new organizations may feel a need to move gingerly into two types of appraisal for nonunionized employees, beginning with a system that is oriented toward development. This system can be used for getting managers acquainted with the rudiments of preparing for, giving, and following up on the control of work assignments, thereby using the job content itself as a vehicle for employee development. This approach is based on the idea of "stretch," that is, helping employees learn how to fulfill work assignments and gradually to become knowledgeable about all aspects of the job. Employees can be taught the simpler aspects of the job initially and gradually given assignments in the more difficult phases of the work. In this way, they can be tested, challenged, and stretched to become fully competent in the range of work content in the jobs to which they are assigned. Also, if an employee is found to be incapable of stretching his abilities to the full extent inherent in the job, this will be made obvious and decisions can be made as to what would be proper use, training, and guidance for him.

In a word, the main values in starting with the developmental approach are to provide managers with experience in how to use performance appraisals as tools for obtaining results on the job and for relating one on one with employees in order to assist in their development.

The use of appraisals for making decisions about pay adjustments can be started after the business or agency has gained experience using them for development—in a certain sense, when the business is more mature. When appraisals are to be used for pay decisions, the atmosphere in the appraisal interview is likely to be entirely different from that in a developmental interview. Money is such a powerful reward for most employees that discussions about it are likely to make the manager and employee uptight, particularly if the former must deliver bad news and the latter expects it (or receives it when it is unexpected). Merit reviews can be downright nasty and can culminate in various forms of vituperation and unpleasantness, including name calling, crying, or other emotional upheavals, peremptory decisions to quit, and even violence (fisticuffs are not unknown as an outcome for people with short fuses).

Another problem with merit reviews is the card-stacking phenomenon. Managers and employees alike enter the situation defensively, the manager with facts at hand that justify the pay decision and the employee with his reasons for deserving the increase fairly well spelled out. The manager has the cards stacked most strongly and probably will not alter the decision about pay no matter what the employee says. This rigidity is accompanied by the employee's feeling that his pay increase should be at least x percent or y dollars based upon his knowledge of his accomplishments, the cost of living, relativities among employees and peers, or other criteria that may be considered pertinent.

The merit-pay discussion can thus be grubby and extremely unpleasant. Only a mythical Santa Claus is likely to have plenty of goodies to distribute. The typical manager must mete out increases based upon a tight budget, pay policy controls, and something less than Santa Claus' bulging bag of toys.

The stiltedness of the setting can serve the purpose of formal communication about a pay decision poorly and may not be developmental at all. One hopes that it will be somewhat growth-inducing. Employees whose pay adjustment is out of line with expectations may ask what they can do to improve and seriously consider changing their behavior to earn more money. The net result can be developmental motivation. The merit-pay session may not, however, yield this beneficial result—at least, it cannot be depended upon to provide a positive outcome.

Sometimes it is naively argued that the development appraisal should not only focus exclusively upon behavior change but should also rule out any discussion of the monetary aspect. Managers are directed not to discuss money and pay adjustments under any circumstances. Unfortunately, it is not always possible to bifurcate the appraisal process in this way. For example, once the manager tells an employee that he is carrying out most of his job duties in a superlative manner, the employee is likely to switch the subject to how this observation on performance will be translated into dollars and cents in the paycheck. It is unrealistic to advise the manager that he should or must not talk about money in the context of developmental appraisal on the grounds that it is inappropriate. The psychological flow of moving from a manager-employee performance appraisal interview supposedly based upon development to one focussed on a pay adjustment decision is natural. This is particularly true if the review is favorable, the employee perceives himself as having worked hard and deserving of a substantial raise, and the manager would like to reward the employee as well as possible within the company's or agency's pay policy guidelines. Yet some organizations inveigh against talking about pay in a developmental appraisal session. They theorize that the session will deteriorate into a contest of wills over pay levels and personality clashes that should be *verboten*.

The main argument of real importance against combining appraisals for pay with appraisals for development is that the former will eclipse the latter in the appraisal session and that the manager will structure the remarks about performance solely to those that are consonant with the pay decision. This will result in a prostitution of the developmental discussion so that it buttresses the pay decision and nothing growthful is accomplished. The prostitution has the effect of cancelling the possibility of a meaningful developmental discussion. Of course, there is nothing inevitable about this prostitution for all subordinates in all organizations, but it would be hard to deny that the potential is there.

All the reasoning discussed above leads to the conclusion that for many organizations, it is wise to separate the two types of review—conceptually, temporally, and administratively. But it is possible to combine the two, and this is desirable for mature, sophisticated organizations in which there are numerous managers who are up to speed in appraisal skills and can handle both developmental and compensation topics. In this way they can save themselves time and duplication of systems. The key to this saving is the installation of a viable MBO system, and the manner in which it can be constructed to work for the manager is covered later in the book in Chapters 29 through 41. Such an approach is certainly not for everyone—and this should be read as a major caution—yet where the transition can be made from dual systems to a single one, there are obvious economies and administrative conveniences in doing so.

6

Once a system has been decided upon, apply it for several years; in other words, don't tinker with the system annually.

A WIT ONCE COMMENTED that the last act of a dying organization is to rewrite the rule book. By the same reasoning, the last act of a moribund performance appraisal system is the guaranteed annual manual, that is, a new form, set of ground rules, and minor procedural change that must be mastered anew by every manager every year. Is it any wonder that managers recoil at the appraisal system with which they must live?

Many managers give performance reviews reluctantly, and their reservations become pandemic when the personnel/human-resource specialists tinker with the system each year in trivial ways.

In brief, *no* performance review system should be installed until the apparently best system tailored to the special requirements of a business or agency is created, fashioned, and installed in the organization together with appropriate training packages for managers who must live with the system. This guideline seems very obvious but the opposite practice (that is, annual tinkering) seems to prevail among those large companies and agencies that have gone in for performance appraisals.

Once installed, no well-conceived system should be altered until a quantum improvement can be made. Small changes in procedures and formalities should be kept in abeyance until there are enough of them in addition to conceptual improvements that would justify "changing the system." Careful attention to alteration may win over reluctant managers who are dubious as to whether personnel/human-resource specialists know for sure what they are doing in structuring performance appraisal systems.

Put another way, managers should accept with open minds their role in carrying out performance reviews in a well-conceived performance appraisal system. It is important to note that an appraisal system is a "thing" (administrative tool) created by the personnel/human-resources manager for the employing organization to assist operating line and staff managers in appraising people. If there is no such system, the appraisal of employees could be based upon buddy-buddy systems, favoritism, the manuevering of organizational power blocs of "ins" and "outs" or "us" versus "them," and similar criteria.

Nowadays these politically based or personal-based systems could run foul of the law and surely would allow prejudice to reign rather than equal employment opportunity. Also, such systems would be destructive of pay-for-performance concepts. Thus, a well-conceived appraisal system is always a step in the right direction and permits the formalizing of what we have seen exists informally wherever people live and work together: distinguishing among human performances. Managerial support for sound systems can best be won if the performance appraisal system is stabilized and changed only when modifications are truly warranted. An incidental—but important—result of judicious change can be to improve the reputation of the personnel/human-resource specialists in building sound systems that, as a consequence, deserve support.

We do not oppose change. Managers will, and should, oppose capricious tinkering with the performance appraisal system. One of a manager's most unpleasant encounters can be with a taunting employer who disparages the company's or agency's seemingly aimless guaranteed annual manual and performance review ritual. Such taunts invite managerial acquiescence, which has a further insinuating effect on the performance appraisal system.

As for the HR/PMD, it must clearly recognize that the "thing" (that is, the performance appraisal system) it has created for the employing organization is an important part of the managerial infrastructure. The system should be neither overcontrolled nor changed without managerial and employee participation. The HR/PMD should avoid being seen as a traffic cop who polices the system by making minor annual changes that are monitored in a picayune way. An important goal in any company or agency should be for the employees and managers to "own" their performance appraisal system. It will be difficult for them to do so if it is an unstable entity.

7

Base all performance appraisal systems on job descriptions that are "hunting licenses" or "jurisdictions" and not "straightjackets."

J OB DESCRIPTIONS are often like a meatloaf: a little of this and a bit of that baked together. The ones that are based upon half-baked job analyses are likely to come under governmental scrutiny in the event of an EEO lawsuit. It therefore behooves management to analyze the tasks and duties it considers integral in job content and to evaluate employee job performance on the basis of an adequate and realistic understanding of what the job entails. More and more employees resent and resist performance appraisals that are based on unclear job duties or duties that were never intended to be included in the job in the first place. Duties in some jobs change over time; therefore, it is vital that job descriptions be kept up to date. It is primarily the manager's duty to see that the job descriptions of the employees who report to him accurately reflect the work being done.

The personnel/human-resource specialists in a business or agency are charged to maintain the overall job evaluation and performance review systems *as systems*. But this maintenance task cannot be carried out well unless managers bring changes to the attention of the personnel/human-resource specialists who may then audit the appropriateness of the job description for the work actually being performed by employees.

Unfortunately, orderly and methodical audits of the validity of job descriptions are rare indeed in American industry, except in unionized settings where the union typically polices such descriptions carefully. This is the case perhaps because improper classifications when corrected can yield higher rates of pay for union members. Today's counterpart for the nonunion sector is the government's role as police officer for improperly classified, improperly paid, and improperly appraised employees.

While the need for accurate, up-to-date job descriptions is patent, this remark does not imply that jobs should be narrowly defined, deenriched, and nonhuman in their main aspects. On the contrary, the bulk of the job enlargement, job enrichment, and quality-of-work life research completed in recent decades suggests that jobs should be structured on a scale that has an adequate motivational appeal for a work force that expects more from jobs than did our forbears. In respect to performance appraisals, this change in job—and life—satisfactions from work calls for a broader look at jobs than was ever required before.

Managerial, professional, technical, clerical, and office employees resist jobs that are straightjackets and prefer jobs with expandable boundaries and jurisdictions. Some employees want more elasticity or ambiguity than others. For example, many people see job descriptions as hunting licenses and the more aggressive carry this conception to a point where they become empire builders, assuming tasks and duties that greatly aggrandize their work (and make it worth more pay in the scheme of job evaluation). Thus, not all the behavior that we see in organizations is peaceable and contributes to organizational harmony. Some empire builders do so at the expense of others and become bitterly resented as a consequence. But the other side of the coin is not negative. Employees who take an enlarged view of their jobs are likely to become more contented and better performers.

These observations have important implications for performance appraisals. On the one hand, we need to define employee performance expectations and standards within the confines of the up-to-date job description. Yet, the better managers and professionals may be constantly expanding the boundaries of their jobs, thereby making the job description out of synchronization with the actual world of work.

The manager needs to take a dynamic view of the job description and an accurate, current look at specific job duties at any given point in time. The synchronization of the two is often difficult and could lead to manager-employee communication problems which, in the extreme case, might place unlawful demands on a job incumbent. Contemporary insights into human behavior derived from the social sciences would suggest that attempts at synchronization are warranted and should be tried.

The last word on job boundaries is to return again to union views. Although a few unions in America have endorsed quality-of-work life experiments, including job enrichment, the more prevalent union ideology favors building fences around jobs and maintaining narrow jurisdictions in job content. An occasional collective-bargaining agreement will endorse the crossing of skilled trades lines by craftsmen in order to perform work efficiently, without featherbedding. Such an agreement will support something more than an ultranarrow conception of job boundaries. But the prevalent union view is narrow and in opposition to performance appraisal, no matter how well the latter is conceptualized and administered.

8

Forget about applying performance appraisal to unionized employees once they have seniority.

Pᴇʀʜᴀᴘꜱ ᴛʜᴇ ᴘʀᴀᴄᴛɪᴄɪɴɢ ᴍᴀɴᴀɢᴇʀ who has had a great deal of contact with unions believes that it is impossible to involve unions in performance appraisal regardless of the employee's seniority, assuming that unions will reject the concept out of hand. They could also argue that unions in the United States were legitimized under legislation that conceived of them as adversarial by nature. The role of unions is to react to management's acts, challenging those that do not seem consistent with the economic goals of an essentially political bottoms-up organization (namely, the union). Rather than expect a union to be interested in the improvement of performance, one might count on the union to react against any efforts at employee appraisal that might jeopardize the union member's security of employment, chances for a pay increase, or well-being. Unions have a basic function in securing justice at the work place, protecting their members' pride and dignity. Unions reflect this orientation by insisting on the installation

41

of grievance procedures as soon as they can bargain for them after securing managerial recognition.

The Lockheed, New York City, and Chrysler bail-outs show that unions can be made to take an interest in performance and productivity when management's situation is desperate and the alternative is no jobs at all. While the unions still play an adversarial role in an economic crunch, they can be brought around if the stakes are high enough—even to the point of accepting pay cuts and deferrals.

In broad principle, managers should insist on varying the amount of pay for employees based upon their appraised or measured performance. If this prerogative is watered down by collective-bargaining agreements, managers should insist on the right to evaluate employees at periodic dates during the probationary period prior to the time when the employee obtains a date of service for seniority purposes and can thereafter be discharged only through "due process" for cause. While few Americans are likely to find "due process" an incongenial concept, in practice it may become an obnoxious burden if policed by a union that unreasonably challenges managers' attempts to discipline the work force. Thus, employees with seniority may become virtually untouchable for performance failures, and managers may conclude that it is not worth the trouble to try to take corrective action.

In government agencies, for example, it takes a "federal case" with extensive documentation of performance failures, managerial attempts to rehabilitate and counsel the employee in question, and the like to prove cause for dismissal (and even then the discharge may not stick). Naturally, not all performance failures should culminate in capital punishment in employment (that is, dismissal) but such lesser penalties as one-or three-day layoffs or pay docking may be equally time-consuming and enervating for managers. The will to bear these burdens, however, must be found or management's right to manage human resources can be seriously undermined.

In respect to unionized employees who have seniority, managers are best advised to forget the possibility of formal performance reviews. Of course, the union contract may ban them, and that would limit what policy management can apply. When due process in employment is followed, however, managers need to be aware of performance on the job as the basis for taking action against employees.

It is important also to remember that recent court decisions in the United States have awarded large settlements to non-unionized longer-service employees who were fired capriciously, ruling that dismissals should be for just cause. Promises made in company or agency personnel handbooks (and even oral promises made by managers) are starting to be regarded by courts of law as contracts that preclude dismissal except for "just cause." There have even been cases in which employees have won the right to seek punitive damages on top of lost wages.

Much litigation can be expected over discharges for alleged poor performance in future years with arguments centering in perceptions of performance, what constitutes capricious termination, and the element of just cause. All of these are issues that are outside of Title VII and EEO, but they have theoretical grounding in the Fourteenth Amendment to the Constitution.

The upshot of these legal developments is to place the spotlight once again in the 1980s on the performance-versus-seniority issue in human-resource management. The practicing manager is probably aware that our society is continuing the trend toward greater job security and tenure of employment that was planted by craft and industrial unions in the 1920s and 1930s and by professional associations in the 1960s and 1970s. The effect of this trend is to limit the use of performance as a criterion in decisions that affect human resources.

The above discussion assumes that management bargains with a strong union and does business in a stable product or service market or the burgeoning public sector. Weak unions may present a less formidable adversary in bargaining over the applicability of performance appraisals. Where markets are volatile, management may feel less inclined to insist on great freedom of action in human-resource matters. Relative bargaining power as well as litigation must be considered in whatever strategy is formulated concerning the planning, control, and administration of performance appraisals.

9

Do not rely on formal performance appraisals to do the entire job in communicating on performance; day-to-day informal contacts must do the bulk of the job.

If a manager is not sensitive to the needs, skills, attitudes, abilities, and levels of knowledge of his subordinate employees, he will find himself having problems sooner or later in interpersonal relationships. Indeed, management has been defined by many experts as obtaining results through people. So far in this book we have been emphasizing "obtaining results" as a consequence of human performance. We now switch for the moment to the "through people" aspect of the simple but accurate definition of management offered above.

The manager should regard employees who report to him as extensions of himself who have been hired, trained, and paid to attain results. In stating this concept, there is no implication that employees are mere hired hands. Tasks are delegated to employees to be performed, and collaborative efforts are coordinated by the manager. In this perspective we see people doing work and delegation as the mechanism for the orchestration of human effort so that the result is a concert in which the manager wields the baton.

The performance appraisal provides a formal opportunity for the boss and subordinates to stop the concert on occasion so that they may evaluate how the subordinate is playing his part. The formality of the performance appraisal interview, the actual paperwork processed, and the give and take in the interview signify that something of organizational importance is, one hopes, taking place. If all goes well in the performance appraisal interview—for example, if the boss and the subordinate are both prepared, their oral communication is good, and the job duties and results are clear—then conceivably the resultant appraisal has a fair chance of being successful and meeting its purposes. As described, however, the successful appraisal cannot be expected to do the entire job of communicating on performance.

As a formalization of what has already been communicated in day-to-day encounters between the manager and subordinate, the formal appraisal can then be extremely useful. If day-to-day contacts have been absent and superior-subordinate relations have been remote, then there is a fair probability that the formal review will be unsuccessful, either in total or substantial part. This is the reason why annual performance reviews that are jammed together with all of a manager's subordinates before the end of the year occasionally turn out unfruitful for subordinates and may be viewed as harassment by the manager whose definition of his main responsibility is "seeing that iron is shipped out the back door." Production and sales tasks are of top priority while performance appraisals are seen not as something that helps the manager manage better, but as something that allows the HR/PMD to justify their empire better. Appraisal becomes convoluted and resented.

The roots of the formal appraisal situation should be in the day-to-day, week-to-week, and month-to-month interface between the manager and the subordinate based upon the conduct of assigned tasks. Not all work requires day-to-day contact. Indeed, some tasks are best delegated, and experienced employees are encouraged to check back with the manager only when they need counsel, help in problem solving, or other guidance that can best be furnished by one's organizational superior. Management by exception can be a fitting philosophy in these circumstances. Microscopic supervision would be inappropriate and could be counterproductive for obtaining satisfactory results from the employee.

Individual differences between employees always come into play, of course, in discussions of the individual's preferences concerning how much contact he may desire with his manager. Also, how much experience and training an employee possesses dictates how often the boss should have to check on the quality of performance of any delegated tasks. Neither qualification, however, invalidates the principle that the quality of the manager-subordinate relationship as it exists informally affects the chances that the formal performance appraisal interview will have a successful outcome.

To obtain results through people, the manager must know the employees who report to him, must communicate clearly with them, and must know how to handle the formal appraisal interview itself. There should, as stated earlier, be no surprises in the formal interview—at least no major surprises. The formal setting should be used merely to recapitulate and reiterate what took place informally over the days, weeks, months, and year. Such a formal review then places on the record what the employee has long hungered to hear officially: how well he is doing.

Once the record is laid open, explained, reviewed, and debriefed, plans can be made for the employee's development during the next year. The manager-subordinate encounter can be open, authentic, growthful, confronting, and developmental. It may or may not get into pay matters (as discussed previously). The interview is likely to end on a positive note: the boss will return to his job and the subordinate to his, both feeling good about the experience and fully prepared to go about their day-to-day work and resume their informal give and take at the workplace as problems arise in the conduct of work activities.

If the informal relations are so good, what is to be gained by a formal review? The nature of the performance is made a matter of record, the manager and subordinate have communicated, the planning and controlling of assigned work has been examined as a process, and the employee has satisfied his desire to know how he is doing. Perhaps of even greater importance for overall management is that the manager has acted to obtain results through people by using a powerful tool available to him of which there is no functional equivalent—namely, the formal performance appraisal.

10

Review performance formally at least once per year—and whenever there has been a repetition of negative employee behavior.

THERE IS NO MAGIC NUMBER to dictate the timing of performance appraisals. Inasmuch as budgets are based on fiscal or calendar years, corporations engage in annual profit planning, employees hope for pay increases every twelve months, and January to December constitutes a natural circadian cycle, we think performance reviews should be given once per year. The date of the review could be the anniversary of the employee's employment date or could be staggered throughout the year to be made administratively convenient for the manager. Probationary employees should be given reviews at intervals of 60, 90, 120, or 180 days and annually thereafter. The manager should feel no reluctance to conduct a review whenever there has been seriously negative employee behavior, particularly if it is repeated or continual. By the same token, there is no reason why strongly positive or creative employee behavior should not culminate in a performance review "for the record." The performance review is not by nature a punitive tool, although it may be seen that way if its main application is to document negative performance for the record and lead eventually into a disciplinary hearing and punishment. Conceptually, it is better to consider the developmental purpose of the performance appraisal as a preferable take-off point.

When employee performance is never formally reviewed, or is carried out irregularly, or stretched into every two or three years, or whenever the manager gets around to it, the idea of a performance appraisal system becomes a mockery. Employees like regular feedback, and it is as fitting for them to have periodic report cards as it is for students, although it may sound rather flippant when the matter is stated in this way. Nevertheless, without the regularity of feedback and knowledge of work results, an employee's hunger to know where he stands is not satisfied. He may lose his sense of purpose, will to perform, satisfaction with the job, and interest in staying with the employer.

In view of what has been discussed in this book, it may be obvious that the concentration of the performance feedback content should be on the job-related behavior of the employee, not on his personality. For example, consider the employee whose performance has fallen off after a long period of satisfactory work behavior. In this instance, the manager should explain to the employee why the performance review session has been scheduled. He should ask the employee if he is experiencing any particular problems that may be contributing to the performance decrement, and he (the manager) must pay close attention to the employee's response. The manager should determine if there are circumstances under his control causing the employee problems that he can help to alleviate. The manager and employee should agree on actions that can be taken by each and, finally, set a time at which they can meet again to discuss progress and improvements.

This problem-oriented approach minimizes defensiveness on the part of each of the participants. No attacks are made on the employee's self-esteem. His felt need to justify substandard performance is minimized. The manager, by framing his comments in goal-oriented terms, can avoid the uncomfortable role of playing God (a problem to which I return later in the book). What is expected from the employee is clearly stated. Further appeal to the previously articulated difficulties leading to the initial problem or problems will no longer be possible (assuming they were properly identified during the earlier scheduled performance review session). Also, the employee is made aware that his improvement will indeed be rechecked at some specified date.

Clearly, training on how to provide specific problem-oriented feedback sessions in a constructive context is required as a part of the overall effort for developing managerial competence in the conduct of appraisals. The practice of "back slapping" may contribute to employee morale but may also perpetuate particular aspects of work behavior that are improperly performed. If a specific problem or task was well handled, the manager needs to recognize this. Generalized feedback can be misleading, particularly if the sessions for communicating it are few and far between.

In order to provide specific feedback clearly on areas where performance improvement is required, the manager should concentrate on no more than three topics. This magic number consists of a manageable amount of information for most employees. More feedback may decrease the employee's motivation to improve his performance. In addition, training on mutual problem solving may be required, which places a burden on each of the parties involved as well as on the employer who must provide it.

Of course, the manager must also know how to be specific, which requires awareness of one's own skill in oral communication. The manager should state *what it is* about the employee's job performance that is lacking and *what it is* that has been observed. These comments should be behavioral in their reference. The manager should also offer suggestions for improvement, as well as allowing the employee opportunities to generate solutions to the problem or problems.

Above all, the manager should avoid attacks on the employee's personality. The focus at all times should be on problems, the specific goals to be obtained, and the actions required to reach them—and away from blame and blame-fixing witch hunts.

There is, of course, nothing inevitable about a downward spiral in employee motivation, but the gains to be realized from a well-designed and well-administered system of performance appraisal are indisputable. Modern large-scale work organizations are loath to rely on informal appraisals that are haphazardly communicated and totally unmonitored. The success of formal systems depends on the enthusiastic support of managers who use performance appraisals as a scheduled way of running their jobs, not as sops for keeping the in-house personnel/human-resources experts happy. The best way— and a natural one—to use the performance appraisal is in an annual cycle that is in harmony with the budget, profit plan, and fiscal or business calendar.

11

**Write the appraisal—do not rely on unrecorded
discussions.**

From everything said so far, it should be obvious that informal oral evaluations do not meet the requirements of a formal performance appraisal of on-the-job behavior. Again,
there can be no appraisal system worthy of the name that is not
written and not recorded. Yet there is no contradiction between urging the manager to observe employees at work informally and furnishing them with constructive feedback on the
scene *and* advocating a formal system.

The informal and formal should be mutually supportive. A
formal system whereby the manager is judge and rater and the
employee is defendent and ratee can be as unsuccessful as an
informal, loose-as-a-goose, unrecorded method.

Occasionally, one meets a manager who hates to keep
records and prefers a neat, free-and-easy, folksy relationship
with his subordinates. He feels that the former (record keeping) will inhibit obtaining the latter. Indeed, it might, but
there is no reason why it must.

A record of performance that goes back a year or two (or maybe three) is necessary, especially if one considers the possibility that, for example, a manager might die and that his memory will, perforce, die with him. While a small gap in performance appraisal records is not going to jeopardize the viability of most firms and agencies, there is no need to tolerate such a gap based upon the employee relations theory of the free-and-easy, folksy manager who rejects the concept of written appraisals.

12

Require the human resource (personnel) management department (HR/PMD) to keep a file of performance appraisals for no more than two years—ideally no more than one year—and purge all ancient history!

Mᴀɴᴀɢᴇʀs ɴᴇᴇᴅ ᴀ ғᴏʀᴍᴀʟ ᴇᴍᴘʟᴏʏᴇᴇ ʀᴇᴄᴏʀᴅs sʏsᴛᴇᴍ but they need only one. In the light of privacy legislation and freedom of information laws, businesses and government agencies should not tolerate double, triple, and multiple records of employee history, performance, potential, pay, and the like.

The HR/PMD should be the repository of employee records of all kinds, and there should be only one set of records! Sometimes there are multiple sets of records: those that are correct and official, which the employee cannot and does not see, and those that are incorrect, unofficial, and open to the public. This type of chicanery is not only deplorable as a matter of human-resources policy but is unlawful in states with privacy laws.

Sometimes managers keep parallel or abbreviated records for their own convenience, with no sinister purposes in mind.

This practice should be discouraged even though it might not be intended as a way to circumvent the law.

By and large, performance appraisals are relevant for sets of managers and subordinates and meaningful as long as employees work for the same manager. Records should not be kept forever, and a year or two of past history generally should be sufficient. In those instances in which old performance appraisals are being maintained as documentation for an employee whose performance and behavior have severely declined, those records should be maintained for the purpose at hand. Otherwise, there is no need to keep such extensive histories on all employees.

In a broader sense, in pace-setting organizations the bulk of performance and disciplinary problems are in all likelihood confined to a relatively small percentage of the work force, perhaps only 3 to 5 percent of all employees. Thus, there is no reason to maintain lengthy performance records on the other 95 to 97 percent.

There is yet another reason for not keeping records on all employees for years past. When employee performance problems appear, they should be dealt with quickly, humanely, and with an eye toward helping the individual to grow. The needs of the business or agency should be paramount but organizational due process should be adhered to in dealing with the problem performer.

It is a poor managerial approach for the manager to sweep the performance problem under the rug, hide the problem from others, or hope that it will somehow go away. It is also deplorable for a manager to write up the problem employee's performance in glowing terms in the hopes that some other manager will hire him away or want him for a promotional vacancy. The very worst solution is simply to tolerate the poor performance, to ignore it. The manager may be scheduled to move on in his career and will leave the problem of the poor performer to his successor rather than face up to it. This is nothing but a cheap act of managerial cowardice, an evasive measure that a performance appraisal system cannot tolerate.

Long-simmering performance problems exist primarily because managers do not accept and confront their employee performance appraisal responsibilities. Often, a long record of poor employee performance cannot be documented from the files because cowardly managers never inserted the proper information in the records initially. Thus, it becomes difficult to prove incompetence from the files, so why keep them?

Ideally, managers should call the shots as they see them at the annual performance appraisal and call performance problems in written form to the attention of the HR/PMD so that they can get into the act at an early stage and bring the relevant staff services to bear either on improving the employee's performance in his present job or helping to place him where he can perform, even if that involves the occasional use of outplacement.

An open, honest, authentic performance review properly followed up by the manager and HR/PMD is far preferable to wool gathering from hoary old records long after the fact of persistently unsatisfactory job conduct. The chances are that the merino gathered from old records is not going to be worth much anyway.

As we have seen, courts are taking an increasingly dim view of dismissing long-service employees as incompetent, especially when it would appear that management was guilty of not taking timely action to correct alleged performance deficiencies many years before. Employees are thought to have tenure and property rights in the jobs that they have held for many years and for which there is no documentation of performance inadequacies. This tenure and property right cannot be peremptorily taken away.

Insofar as employee performance is often in the eye of the beholder, it seems that perceptions are crucial in the area of just cause for dismissal for inadequate performance. The best policy for the business or agency is prompt identification, and for the manager, prompt action. Businesses are not run backwards from the records but forwards, based upon the observable dynamics of today. The same is true in administering performance appraisals.

Keep the files lean and relevant.

The HR/PMD should do a proper job of auditing and maintaining the real records. It behooves managers not to have parallel records that could be misconstrued from a legal standpoint. While there is no objection to the manager's recording observations on employee behavior during the year so that a factual foundation is prepared for the conduct of performance appraisals and their write-up, managers should not embellish these observations so that they become parallel files and are given more credence than records maintained by the HR/PMD.

13

While acknowledging that the appraisal itself should be "owned" by the appraiser and appraisee, require the HR/PMD to spot-check appraisals after the fact.

THE MANAGER SHOULD CONSIDER the performance appraisal interview as the heart of the appraisal process itself. The interview brings together the boss and subordinate in a formal setting and consists of both "content" and "process." The content should focus upon the work of the employee and should include any other factors that enter into the employee's goals and duties. For example, if the subordinate supervises the work of others, the business or agency may expect him to fulfill EEO goals when hiring new employees, or to demonstrate his ability in developing subordinates, or to give special attention to the implementation of a program that is being emphasized by the employer, or to use ethical means for implementing ends. Job content consists, then, of specific goals and duties as well as any other special tasks the employer may choose to add and to emphasize in particular.

To the extent that the contents of the appraisal reflect an accurate job analysis, questions of the validity of the performance appraisal are greatly reduced. Naturally, face validity (the surface appearance that the appraisal write-up makes sense) engenders ownership by the appraiser and appraised employee. But demonstrated content validity is necessary to refute equal opportunity charges that the performance appraisal system is subjectively based. Without the required documentation that an accurate job analysis has been completed, the appraisal device will probably result in unfavorable court rulings.

The content of the appraisal should be perceived by both the manager and subordinate, the appraiser and appraisee, as accurately reflecting the tasks of the subordinate. The agreement between the two lays a factual foundation from which performance can be discussed. The two could in this way "own" the appraisal, that is, consider it validly based.

It is to be hoped that the process by which the interview is conducted will then move forward in a way that allows participative give and take between the boss and employee. It takes great skill in the process phase of the interview for the appraisal to culminate in a conclusion that both participants will perceive as positive. (We come back to many of these process issues in some of our subsequent guidelines. Suffice it to say here that good process working with mutually understood content enable the heart to perform its vital circulatory function in appraisal.)

Strangely, in many organizations the appraisal is "owned" by neither the appraiser nor the appraisee. In fact, there are still businesses and agencies that treat appraisals as report cards made to the HR/PMD by managers and are never seen by the employee. In these cases, there are no appraisal interviews. In many states the employee now has the right to request a personal look at what is filed as a report on his performance in his personnel jacket or on the computer and has the right to submit additional facts to correct or rebut the record.

Perhaps the worst sham in appraisal is when the boss completes an appraisal form and sends it to the HR/PMD indicating that a performance review interview has taken place when in fact none has. This lie rules out any possibility of ''ownership'' of the appraisal and is worse than report cards because the deception amounts to thwarting established managerial policy on the administration of appraisals. There are many reasons (or alibis) why a manager might engage in this deception, including being too busy, unwilling, apprehensive, and fearful, or opposed to appraisals. None of these excuses justifies deceit but the latter is hardly an unknown phenomenon.

Clearly, the HR/PMD should spot-check appraisals after the fact to determine how well they report on the content and process of the appraisal interview. Auditing a sample should provide insight into whether the appraisal was given and generally whether content within the job description was discussed. But it would be naive to accept the reports at face value. The HR/PMD may never know whether the written form actually covered the content and what concretely transpired in the interview. It will learn even less about the quality of the process from a review of the sample of filed forms.

Spot-checks can be followed by telephone calls to managers and subordinates to inquire how they perceived the direction and outcome of the interview. Also, routine organizational attitude surveys may pick up information of the perceived adequacy of appraisals, particularly from a processual standpoint. Exit interviews may add further information about the administration of appraisals.

The behaviors of the manager are probably far more important than the after-the-fact audits made by the HR/PMD. Managers can act before the fact to assure that the appraisal interview is a worthwhile experience and can conduct themselves during the interview based upon the dynamics that emerge there to guide the session toward a constructive developmental conclusion. Managerial actions and communication with the subordinate are important keys to ownership of the appraisal.

14

An appraisal should cover one side of an 8½ x 11 sheet of plain paper which is simple to read and understand. Longer ones are not useful and should be avoided.

Earlier in the book the ideal type of performance appraisal was presented (see Figure 4.1). This form is clearly simple. It is not necessarily simple, however, to prepare it prior to a performance appraisal interview. In fact, it can be very difficult for a manager to draw it up if he has trouble thinking analytically and clearly of what he wants his people to accomplish. The form emphasizes analysis rather than procedure or mindless following of a method, such as checking the judgmental boxes on a graphic rating scale (as in Figure 2.1).[6]

The manager will never be able to prepare a meaningful performance appraisal unless he has skill in planning and controlling assigned work. Managers who define their work as fire fighting and see their tasks as a series of unpredictable and uncontrollable events are likely to see their subordinates as equally caught up in a tempestuous, directionless world.

The planning- and control-oriented manager will like an easy-to-read and understandable appraisal format and will be willing to roll up his sleeves to embark on the hard analytical work required to breathe life into the simple form we advocate using.

How does a nonanalytically inclined manager react to a simple form? He is likely to feel frustrated about coming to grips with what he is expected to appraise and how he is expected to do so. Obviously, some of the forms of training on the administration of performance review by managers which are discussed below (in Chapters 19 through 22) can be helpful to the nonanalytically inclined manager. He must be provided high-quality training and must want to use the performance appraisal format. If he would rather check a graphic rating scale or skip performance appraisal altogether, then he may be hard to bring on board in the company's appraisal effort.

While the one-page form suggested in Figure 4.1 may be useful and desirable for most managers, there are those who may need an extra page or more to give reviews to their employees. There is nothing wrong in this.[7] To prevent it would be irrational. But long complex forms should be avoided for any number of obvious reasons. Long forms may turn off the busy manager, and they probably focus upon both the crucial and the trivial aspects of the appraisee's work without making a proper distinction between the two. Long forms that are structured as checklists may be more acceptable. But they will probably be less valid because they may not capture very accurately the subtleties of the jobs of a variety of subordinates. It is difficult to press the duties of a multitude of employees in a diversity of jobs into a universally applicable checklist and have it turn out as valid or even useful.

In the search for the Holy Grail of performance appraisal forms over the decades, much attention has been given to the length of forms, the artwork on them, the books containing the forms, training paraphernalia, color variations, paper quality, and other such minutiae and gimmicks that hype the latest approach. Perhaps this search for prettiness and eye appeal is to be commended but to commend it would cause us to focus on trivia that are of no conceptual importance. Moreover, to concentrate too much on such trivia is to lose sight of the important business we are about—which is *not* the employment of the world's commercial artists.

15

All appraisals should be reviewed by the boss
and the boss' boss before the actual interview.

THE WISE MANAGER prepares the performance appraisal form
in draft and submits it to his organizational superior for a
review. In this way multiple judgment is used and the
organizational superior of the appraisee two levels up has a
chance to learn about what the employee is doing. This insight
may shed light into how the appraiser functions as a manager
of human resources without intruding into the relationship
between the manager and his people.

Another benefit derived from review of the appraisal by
two levels of management before the appraisal interview takes
place is that it may improve the quality of the appraisal write-
up. The review can be used as an opportunity to train the
manager in how to evaluate performance in the event that the
manager's organizational superior is seasoned and interested
in helping his subordinate manager. The manager's boss may
also be able to avoid EEO problems and prejudice that could

67

have inadvertently crept into an appraisal that was prepared by a relatively inexperienced manager.

There are other alternatives that are sometimes suggested to inject multiple judgments into the appraisal. First, it has been proposed that the appraisee's peers probably know a great deal about his performance and that this information should be secured and assessed. Why not? The U.S. armed services have made great use of peer or buddy appraisal, particularly in officer-training programs. The stories stemming from screw-your-buddy week (as these peer appraisals are sometimes known because they often take place in a compressed period, such as the last week of training) are both ludicrous and instructive.

Peers, however, may have views about appraisee's behavior that may be suppressed whenever the appraisee deals with his boss, the manager. Some people are poor peers but brilliant apple polishers, while other people do not impress the boss as much as they do their peers. Peer appraisals will normally bring information about these discrepancies to the surface. Peers may be more severe critics of one another than the bosses of the same employees would be.

Another alternative is for the employee to initiate action on his own performance appraisal by completing a written draft report to be sent to his manager for study prior to the performance appraisal interview. The manager reads the draft, prepares written comments on it, and returns it to the subordinate. The two then meet in the appraisal interview and jointly draft the performance appraisal. (This step could be avoided if the boss simply studies the subordinate's performance review draft and then drafts his own report based upon not only what the subordinate prepared but also the boss' understanding of how well the subordinate met his assigned objectives.) Regardless of the procedure used, the method appears to be participative and has potential applicability if its users are willing to invest the time and energy necessary to make it work and have the skills to communicate effectively in writing. The method has, however, apparently not caught on to any appreciable extent.

Peer appraisals and employee-initiated reviews can be used by the manager in order (1) to tap all information available about an appraisee, and (2) to make the process as participative as possible. These techniques by no means rule out appraisals made jointly by the boss and the boss' boss and should be seen as adjuncts that supplement the boss and boss' boss method advocated in this book.

16

Employees should be asked to sign each
performance appraisal but should be allowed to
refuse to do so.

Once the performance appraisal has taken place, the
employee should be asked to sign the form. If he refuses to do
so, this fact should be noted on the form, and the HR/PMD
should follow up meticulously to find out the reasons for the
refusal. It perhaps goes without saying that the manager
should not forge the employee's signature or become coer-
cive about obtaining a signature. The employee's refusal to
sign should simply be noted. Once the form is received in this
condition by the HR/PMD, the latter should audit what happened.

We have been progressing through a logical flow of events
in which the performance appraisal interview takes place and
is concluded. An interview that results in an employee's
refusal to sign the form (or results in his written statement of
disagreement with the appraisal) should signal to the HR/
PMD that there has been no closure on the appraisal.
Somewhere the give and take between the manager and the

subordinate broke down, and the employee has the guts—or is sufficiently foolhardy—to challenge the boss (and even the boss' boss, if he countersigned). Refusal cases of this type are likely to be extremely infrequent (and, incidentally, should not be expected to be frequent if the organization is doing a good job in operating its appraisal system).

In addition to being a safety valve for the employee and a flag to the HR/PMD, the requirement that the employee sign the form probably heads off situations wherein managers send completed appraisal forms to the HR/PMD attesting that reviews were held when they actually were not. Aside from the possibility of forgery—which would be rare and should be significantly punished when discovered because it is an intolerable breach of integrity—the signature of the employee (or his written refusal to sign) should indicate that some kind of performance appraisal interview took place. The content and process of the problematic interview can later be investigated and corrective action can be taken.

When the boss' boss is required to have a role in the performance appraisal of employees two levels below him, refusals can provide a communication channel that is well worth building and maintaining. The option of refusal to sign creates a mechanism much like an expedited grievance procedure, which should be particularly useful in a nonunionized setting where the alternative complaint review system (if there is one) may not function very effectively.

Recently, the courts have begun to take an interest in whether or not the boss' boss reviews the appraisal. An apparent implication of this interest is that the courts favor two levels of review because they may reduce the possible bias of a one-level review and the exercise of personal prejudice.

17

The HR/PMD should study completed appraisal forms from departments to discern trends in toughness (severity), easiness (leniency), bias, and perfunctory administration: to oversee pride and prejudice.

We HAVE REPEATEDLY SUGGESTED that the success of any performance appraisal system depends on how well the manager handles himself within the system. Being people, managers have great individual differences in their ability to work with the system as appraisal givers and receivers.

As givers of appraisals, some managers can be very tough. We need not go into the psychodynamics of why some managers are lenient and others severe in their judgments of subordinates. The fact is variability caused by individual differences. The result can be great inequity.

We live in an era in which equal opportunity has been strongly emphasized in public policy as an antidote for discrimination on the basis of race, ethnic origin, sex, age, and handicap. We have had much discrimination that should have been extirpated decades ago, but it was not.

Equal opportunity needs to be juxtaposed against the concept of unequal pay for unequal work in proportion to the inequality. We know that levels of employee performance differ, and few if any American managers argue for equality of pay for all. Most want pay to be varied according to performance. But how can this be done if manager A's expectation of satisfactory performance is so high that none of his subordinates is considered adequate? How can we explain the dramatic improvement in the performance of manager A's subordinates when manager B takes over his department and evaluates the same employees one or two notches higher? If the people remain the same and perform the same tasks for both manager A and manager B, why is there a dramatic increase in the ratings? Setting aside a minor time-maturation variable, the explanation may be that manager A is severe and manager B is lenient. How defensible are these rating variations in a court of law? Courts are likely to take a dim view of inconsistency in ratings, especially if the appraisal does not control subjectivity and the interjection of prejudice.

Problems of leniency and severity have been identified since the first days when performance appraisals were used in American industry early in the twentieth century. When graphic scales first came into vogue, the two problems became obvious.

Scaling is very judgmental; when untrained managers use rating scales, their prejudices have free reign. In fact, some of the early history of merit rating was devoted to coping with these two problems. For example, an early response to the problem was to force managers to distribute the ratings over the ranges of the scales so as to conform to a bell curve or normal distribution. This solution (called forced distribution) gave little or no cognizance to the fact that managers might, in reality, have subordinates who are indeed excellent performers and deserve to be rated high on the scales. Similarly, other managers might have a variety of mediocre and poor performing subordinates and should have all their employees distributed in the lower part of the scales. Forced distribution did not assist the managers in doing a proper and honest job of appraisal and, if anything, it sowed suspicion as to the meaningfulness of appraisals.

In companies and agencies where employees were well selected and likely poor performers were weeded out during the hiring process, there was no reason to expect a bell-curve distribution of performances. Thus, managers who had made serious efforts at good selection saw the forced distribution of an array of performance appraisals as irrational and inconsistent.

Another aspect of leniency and severity was the "halo effect," also noted for the first time and labeled as such decades ago. The term may seem angelic but it played hob in human-resource management and is synonymous with prejudice because it refers to two types of common prejudgments.

One type of halo involves seizing on a particular (often very minor) aspect of an employee's behavior and generalizing unjustifiably from it. For example, an employee who smokes cigarettes may have a manager who dislikes smoking so much that he considers the employee careless about his health, indifferent to the preferences of others about fouling the air, untidy about how he keeps the appearance of his desk (owing to spilled ashes and cigarette burns on the edges of the desk), smelly, and so on. The other type of halo starts from a general prejudice (which is often vaguely formulated and imprecise) and is applied to every particular aspect of a person. For example, as a youth in boot camp, the manager may have had an ego-shattering experience attributed to a U.S. Marine Corps drill instructor from South Boston. As a result, whenever he reviews the credentials of a job applicant or employee being considered for promotion with a South Boston background, he reacts against these persons on the theory that "nobody from South Boston could be any good." He predicts such a person would be unintelligent, foul-mouthed, rude, overbearing, and objectionable personally in all character and personality traits. To be sure, both types of halo are manifestations of social psychological naivete and both are based upon ignorance.

Also, they are examples of unbridled prejudice used as opportunistic rules of thumb that impede equal opportunity. But they operate extensively to this very day in all walks of life, including among the ranks of well-educated managers in corporations and governmental agencies.

What can be done about stamping out halo, leniency, and severity in making and administering appraisals? There is no easy answer. Some managers can be helped through training which sensitizes them to their rating tendencies and biases. Others may be hard to reach and unwilling to look at themselves honestly in regard to the relative severity of the standards they apply to employees and how their personal halos operate. Some managers may simply feel comfortable with themselves as they are and resist change. They become complacent—perhaps lazy would be more descriptive—and do a perfunctory job in administering appraisals. Perhaps such persons fall into the category of marginal managers or even nonmanagerial material! Today, managers who cannot at least control their prejudices lay a foundation for lawsuits (which their employers are likely to lose) as well as establishing a poor moral reputation in the minds of the public when stories of unlawful employment practices make the pages of the daily newspaper.

The HR/PMD through studies of the information on completed appraisal forms and audits of what is happening can play an important role in protecting individual employee dignity and pride, and control against the untrammeled sway of personal prejudice. The manager himself is in the best position to make corrective actions from HR/PMD audits unnecessary. It should be obvious from what has been stated here and elsewhere that the pivotal role of the manager bears repeating: they can diminish the easiness, toughness, or halo prejudices that can readily come into operation unless conscious attempts are made to control them.

18

Never mail out a performance appraisal self-instruction package to management and hope all will work out well—it won't!

Pity the manager who receives in his in-basket at four-thirty on a Friday afternoon a performance appraisal self-instruction package. What a great way to ruin a weekend, particularly if the package is thick and forbidding and is accompanied by a tight deadline submission date for the manager's appraisals of his current subordinates! Worse, assume the manager is superbusy with "business" assignments, a reluctant appraiser at best, and totally untrained in how to give performance appraisal interviews. Still worse, assume he has experienced ugly clashes in the past during performance reviews he was obliged to stumble through and begrudges every minute spent on any human-resource programs.

The picture of the manager contemplating his performance appraisal interview tasks may be painted happily or gloomily, but it is not likely ever to be a joyous one when a complex package is mailed out and the HR/PMD naively hopes for the best. Unfortunately, mail-outs are very common in companies and agencies in the United States because top management refuses to spend the money needed to help managers learn how to give an effective performance appraisal. Even when the money is made available, managers will have myriad reasons for not taking the time to attend training sessions on the subject. The problem is like the chicken-and-egg conundrum and we return to try to solve it in the following pages.

It must be stated, however, that the manager who receives a package in the mail should clearly—vehemently if necessary—make his views known about being asked to implement a procedure or task for which he has not been trained. This is especially true in the case of appraisals, for the road to utopia in this field has been paved with a history of gimmicky changes, increasingly complicated forms, poor conceptualization, and loads of almost incomprehensible jargon about psychological aspects of the process. Companies and agencies that tinker annually with the forms often have no notion of how much antipathy they generate among managers when they ship out their guaranteed annual manuals to unprepared managers.

Self-instruction in performance appraisal seems to be the poorest imaginable approach to teaching the subject. There is simply too much at stake in the process to think that it can be handled by cognitive learning, that is, merely by reading about it. To be sure, the experienced manager who has had some success with performance appraisal writing, interviews, and follow-up, learned through either formal training or trial and error in working with the process in previous employment with another company may be able to read a self-instruction package and figure out how to translate it into action. His main problems in acceptance of the package and the administration of it would go back to any personal resistance he might have. But the inexperienced manager who has never been on the giving end of appraisals will have serious problems proceeding and can try in good faith to apply the self-instruction but still badly botch his administration of the system.

In a word, the resistances and inadequacies of managers militate against the alleged wisdom of a mail-out to save time and money. Top management's hopes will be doomed sooner or later. The history of introducing, withdrawing, and reintroducing performance appraisal systems throughout American industry and government reflects in many cases a poor introduction and explanation of performance appraisals to managers at the outset. The undulations of performance appraisal systems could have been substantially reduced, if not actually eliminated, by introduction of the systems from the top of the organization down, buttressed by training *and* by a decision to stick with feasible systems for several years until the bugs were worked out. Such a comment is more than a statement of faith. It highlights top management's need to be sensitive to the manager who does the appraising, and emphasizes the need to provide this manager, in a stable way, with the tools that *he* needs to perform his own job as an administrator!

19

Prepare detailed two- or three-day performance appraisal workshop/seminars, and require all managers who give appraisals to attend them.

Turning from ineffective mail-outs to effective training, we need not distinguish in any detail between the content of training offered to experienced and to inexperienced managers. Suffice it to say that even experienced managers need booster shots of training whenever major parts of the performance appraisal system are changed. Experienced managers who are deficient as appraisers may need coaching by their organizational superiors or help offered through formal training programs focussing upon interviewing techniques, methods for setting and measuring objectives, and means for developing employees through on-the-job work assignments.

Our concern here is with what the inexperienced manager needs to know fundamentally about performance appraisals in general and about any company's or agency's system in particular. His needs should first be determined so that his input is considered the subsequent building blocks of the basic program which are then best presented in a workshop/seminar atmosphere that has a duration of probably two or three days. Each of the days would involve about eight clock hours of training. Thus, sixteen to twenty-four hours would be devoted to a subject that often receives no attention at all! When we consider what the manager needs to know about performance appraisals and, chances are, he never learns, it becomes even more appalling that the norm of American industry is no training at all!

The content of the basic performance appraisal workshop seminar should normally include:

- The goals of appraisal—why we have it, the strengths and weaknesses of appraisal, and what uses are made of appraisals by the company or agency.
- Appraising the performance of employees—why we focus upon observable behavior, means for establishing measurable goals (and their attainment and shortfalls), and practice in goal setting and measurement.
- Explanation in detail of the component parts of the performance appraisal system(s) used by the employer (complete with question-and-answer sessions regarding the policies, forms, and procedures used).
- Explanation of techniques of interviewing applied to appraisals in a workshop learning atmosphere, including some theoretical material on interviewing principles as well as role plays, case studies, and the dissection of previously used in-house or outside performance appraisal reports (removing, of course, the names of employees and managers).
- Explanation of coaching, follow-up techniques, and methods for developing employees on the job (and through formal training if needed) again together with question-and-answer sessions, role plays, and case studies, as appropriate.

It should be obvious from this listing that even within sixteen to twenty-four hours much is being attempted in a very limited period. Many knowledgeable experts could reasonably argue that it is too much. Interviewing itself, they would say, is worth at least a week's instruction. Recognizing the demands placed on managers' time, others could argue that the practicable limit is such that much worthwhile managerial development must be bob-tailed. Thus, sixteen to twenty-four hours for performance appraisal training would appear to be a practicable limit. (It should be especially noted that no content on salary administration policies, rules, and practices is included in these performance appraisal workshop/seminars.)

In the above discussion of training it is assumed that a competent instructor performs the training and that good-quality training aids are used that seem realistic to the managers. Experienced managers should review the materials to make sure that they are authentic and consistent with top management's policies. All newly appointed managers should receive this basic performance appraisal training soon after their appointment as managers so that they are prepared to handle employee appraisals as scheduled.

The training provided should be mandatory so that no inexperienced manager is allowed to skip it or to rule it out with such excuses as that he has taken course work in industrial and organizational psychology in college. The training should be down to earth and skill oriented, yet provide a sound conceptual foundation for the practices involved. The details of the specific content included are beyond the scope of this book but can easily be worked out by managers, the corporate or governmental in-house experts on performance appraisals, and in-house or outside employee-development and training consultants.

20

Use role playing, television, and experiential techniques to help managers see themselves as evaluators.

Similar to our discussing of the structure of performance appraisal workshop/seminars, in which we kept content general, we also keep the discussion of techniques and training aids general. It must be emphasized, however, that managers like the workshop/seminars on performance appraisals to be specifically grounded in the policies, practices, and procedures of their company or agency. Managers want the content to ring true and to sound practical. Their wisdom concerning the practical problems inherent in appraisal needs to be sought, and when it is properly collected, analyzed, and synthesized, it can go a long way toward creating ownership feelings in regard to the company's or agency's performance appraisal system and the training provided for administering it.

One aspect of content cannot be ignored if we are to do justice to the training aspects of appraisals in this book: that is, that performance appraisal is best taught with experiential learning techniques of all kinds. As indicated above, there is much that can be learned about the theory base for appraisals. This is the cognitive side of the picture. But appraisals call for taking action, learning skills, and communicating with others. This is why role playing using in-house or outside cases, closed-circuit television, and group projects can be used to great advantage. We may wish to enhance sensitivities, show managers how they come across in an artificial appraisal interview, and suggest how they could have handled themselves better. There is no better means for the improvement of skill than skill practice in simulations and in settings that make use of experiential learning and feedback.

Managers need to be encouraged to try experiential learning if they are not familiar with it. Those who dislike getting performance appraisal packages in the mail may not know exactly what makes for a better way of learning about performance appraisals and may think that more cognitive knowledge provided in a lecture/discussion atmosphere would meet their needs. Actually, they require some cognitive knowledge, but more important, they need clinical knowledge that comes from participation in well-designed experiential workshop/seminars.

Managers may resist leaving their jobs for two or three days to attend performance appraisal workshops. They might prefer to attend eight to ten two- or three-hour sessions after working hours or during the latter part of the work day. This type of design may work well where the intensive two- or three-day workshop simply cannot be arranged. If the managers can be immersed in performance appraisal training for eight to ten fairly lengthy sessions, then it may be possible to carry out the training task effectively. The important point is that whatever the scheduling, it is important that the design be participative and experiential and that every newly appointed manager attend.

21

Exclude certain topics from the training on how to give performance reviews, such as issues related to domestic relations, legal and tax affairs, and substance addiction. But encourage managers to make referrals to community resources for employees who apparently need them.

THERE IS A PRACTICAL LIMIT on what can be learned in a two- or three-day workshop/seminar (or the equivalent) in performance appraisal. Managers can learn certain skills in appraisal interviewing at a basic level in the workshop/seminar but cannot acquire any profundity that would suggest that they can function as counselors on the content of domestic relations, legal and tax affairs, or substance addiction.

Unfortunately, people do not enter the world of work as entities who have no ties off the job and no life outside of the factory, office, or agency. They bring their problems to the work place, and these interfere with productivity and performance. The manager is the logical person to turn to for guidance or suggestions if the employee is experiencing anxiety or pain from non-job-related problems.

The wise manager already knows or should learn that off-the-job problems have many facets that even the most well-intentioned altruist cannot identify. Tax problems cannot be solved by suggesting that an employee use the federal long form rather than the short form. Chemical dependency cannot be terminated by a homily on morality. A divorce cannot and should not be encouraged or discouraged or decided upon because the manager had one and thought it worked out well for him. The wise manager simply does not offer superficial bromides no matter how hard an employee pushes for an answer or how badly he seems to need help.

There are companies and agencies today that actually encourage managers during performance interviews or discussions to make preliminary sorties in these areas of controversy if they are observing sudden or uncharacteristic fall-offs in an employee's job performance and the cause seems to be a non-job factor. Perhaps sorties are warranted if they go no further than probing the possible nature of the performance problem. The focal point in performance appraisal, however, should be the employee's performance, not his psyche. There are very serious dangers in amateur psychoanalysis and plumbing psyches. These dangers include the generation of lawsuits by employees, the exacerbation of emotional damages that leave an employee unable to cope, and the provision of irrelevant if not downright harmful advice, however well intentioned it is.

In performance appraisal training managers need to be told company and agency policy on probing some of these proscribed areas. The wise organization simply informs managers about the signs and manifestation of off-the-job factors that could be affecting job performances and encourages managers not to speculate on what in the psyche needs to be dealt with. In brief, the manager has an obligation to observe performance and report it. He has no obligation to be a diagnostician.

The wise organization goes perhaps a step further in providing information by letting the manager know the names, addresses, and phone numbers of community organizations and professionals who are available for consultation by a person who has a problem. The manager is then able to be very specific about community and professional resources and can refer employees to these. The manager can encourage consultation but should leave the decision up to the employee as to whom to call. In this way the employee can feel free to call upon his manager for general and work counseling and select for himself whom he wants to consult professionally over a specific non-job-related problem. The manager is then perceived as a helper with referral knowledge but not as a professional counselor.

Under the demarcation of counseling responsibilities described above, the manager stays in his professional role as a manager whose function is to obtain work results through the efforts of people. Put another way, his profession is human performance management; he should not tread far from it.

We personally deplore the minor trend in American industry for managers to step out of their central role and provide more guidance than they are professionally competent to give. The argument made that managers should be able to counsel in some of the controversial areas mentioned above is a distressing one because it is well intentioned but unintelligent. The argument holds that for many Americans the manager is the *only* resource available that is likely to be given credence and because employees see him as the key to their livelihood. They will pay attention to advice given by the boss and probably take action based on it because their paycheck may depend on it. The same cannot be said about advice given by clergymen, social workers, community volunteers, hot line and crisis centers, and the like. These assertions are difficult to evaluate, but it does seem illogical to push the manager into such deep waters. It is also a pathetic comment on America's social-welfare resources to insist that the only credible helpers and advice givers are in industry and not in the establishment of helping professions. The continuation of an employee's mental health and relief from off-the-job difficulties should not depend upon compliance with nonprofessional advice given by the source of the paycheck. This is the wrong way for companies and agencies to define an important employee relations aspect of the managerial job and should be resisted by the manager.

In another perspective, it should be noted that many work organizations in contemporary America have installed referral programs to which problem performers may be sent for diagnosis. These sources may be internal to the company or agency. Although the employer has no legal or moral right to require the employee to seek help, he can put the employee on notice that the latter's performance is below an acceptable level and that help is both available and convenient. Although a manager or supervisor cannot, in turn, require that a subordinate seek help, a clear statement that if the problem or inadequate performance should persist, stronger action will be taken concerning the employee's job tenure is usually effective in motivating an employee to seek help either internally or externally.

22

Managers can learn to confront, be open and authentic, and develop problem-solving outlooks; but few can become counselors that have the helping professional's touch.

THE PERFORMANCE APPRAISAL WORKSHOP/SEMINAR cannot be all things to all people. But it can make a start toward helping the manager become more open and authentic, and keep a problem-solving outlook in administering performance appraisals.

The manager who regards the performance appraisal system as a facade to hide behind and uses it to whip people and keep them on edge is misapplying a potentially worthwhile tool. Put another way, performance appraisal can be a Theory Y tool used in a Theory Y way or a Theory X tool used in a pseudo-Theory Y or entirely Theory X way. The spirit in which performance appraisal is conducted is the crucial consideration.

Any organization that embarks upon performance review as a human-resource/personnel system should be engaged in the process of creating a way for people to evaluate people that is just, rational, economic, efficient, and lawful. The system should enable managers and employees to encounter one another in a healthy organizational climate.

The vague terms discussed above represent what the installation of a performance appraisal system should inspire in terms of organizational culture. The installation may be imperfect or may fail. Managers may not grow to their potential for openness, authenticity in subordinate relations, and skill in problem solving. In the better installations there will be some growth, perhaps even a great deal.

The installation of an appraisal system will never enable significant numbers of managers to grow into counselors who have the touch of helping professionals, as we have previously noted. They should, however, become more empathetic and sensitive. If, however, one goal of a business or agency is to change the organizational climate, a change in the performance review system should be a part of that effort. In order to heighten the empathy of managers to the fullest a business or agency should embark on an organizational development effort that affects many organizational systems either simultaneously or sequentially to bring about planned change.

The short workshop/seminar can only make a start in the right direction. Expectations of its potential should not be oversold. Unfortunately, this issue is of great fundamental importance because if managers are emotionally blocked, not very socially aware, and insensitive to what they are doing in encounters with employees and specifically in performance appraisal interviews, then even the best designed appraisal system and sound training on its features and administration may not result in a successful application.

It is not practical to suggest that managers need training in all areas of supervising people all at once and to attribute more impact potency to training than can ever be justified. Yet everything in management is interconnected, and there are many building blocks that need to be properly placed in the foundation if a performance appraisal system is constructed to rest on top of them.

The failure of performance appraisal systems in America and the search for the Holy Grail may indeed have less to do with the systems themselves than with the overall preparedness of the managers who are directed to use them! Put another way, maybe the search should be directed not toward better systems but toward how best to prepare system users across the board.

23

Recognize that some managers will never become adept performance appraisers; they don't want to play God.

THERE IS PERFORMANCE APPRAISAL PHILOSOPHY, which we have already discussed, and performance appraisal "theology." The latter has two facets, one of which is discussed next and the other in guideline 24 below.

Managers have many alibis to avoid, postpone, or undependably administer performance appraisals. One excuse goes back to the biblical injunction about passing judgment on one's fellow man (or woman, of course). The manager is, in effect, indicating that he would rather not play God. The summoning of Judgment Day is not for the manager.

This is a difficult phenomenon to evaluate because some managers probably use the refusal to play God as an excuse that masks a different motive in an acceptable form. The manager may find the process personally obnoxious or too costly in time and energy and may not be willing to state this feeling.

There appear to be a number of managers who genuinely

object to playing God. They like being managers and may perform well as experts in their functional areas, but they either trivialize performance appraisals as puerile report cards or berate them on what we are calling "theological" grounds. They probably view work as a means to an end and see no need to use some of the administrative tools that might in some vague way harm subordinates or reduce the size of their pay increments. Also, they may be very empathetic and employee oriented and place a personal type of concept of employee relations ahead of implementing organizational systems. In these instances, the manager perceives himself as engaged in an innocent act of complicity with subordinates, protecting them against the tools of an impersonal business or agency, and HR/PMD in particular. If a person has a job and is performing it tolerably well, then the manager does not feel like playing God.

This theological view has vast implications that can seriously undermine the implementation of performance appraisal and pay-for-performance concepts.

Managers who resist playing God (as they interpret it) may set an unsatisfactory example for their peers who want to use appraisals as planning and control tools in assigning and following up on work done by subordinates. If the appraisal is misused or invidiously played down in one department, then the manager who tries to use the tool properly in another department may be seen as harsh and severe in his approach. The uneven administration of appraisals leads to perceptions of leniency and severity in management which, when broadcast, may create further problems in management's ability to manage as well as laying the groundwork for lawsuits based on the inconsistency of performance standards. This is why it is important to win the support of as many managers as possible for the appraisal system, including, of course, those who oppose it on theological grounds. This, however, is easier said than done.

When managers are advised that their job in appraisal is

not to pass judgment on people and belittle their individual dignity and personal pride, a step toward dealing with the reluctant appraiser can be made. The goal is to look at human output neutrally and not at the input that comprises individuals' identities and uniqueness. The performance appraisal interview looks at behavior and treats employees as human beings who deserve respect, even if their behavior on the job is inadequate or even deplorable.

Performance can theoretically be separated, as we have repeatedly emphasized, from the person, and this is the key to moving away from theological judgment passing. Even the worst performer whose employment is about to be terminated can be handled and treated with dignity. The establishment of outplacement facilities in pace-setting companies and agencies can be interpreted as a contemporary sign of how far organizations are prepared to go to preserve human dignity and smooth difficult career transitions.

24

Recognize that some employees—incidentally, good and bad performers alike—could care less what others think of them; they care only about what God thinks of them, not the boss at work!

THE "THEOLOGICAL" OBJECTION to appraisals has a counterpart in employee opposition which is not unlike managerial opposition in its effects. Consider the following situation (which is *not* a trumped-up example).

The manager has learned how to prepare for and conduct a performance appraisal. He wants to provide successful appraisals. The appraisal form itself is factually correct, based upon observed on-the-job behaviors. The rapport between the manager and subordinate employee is excellent during the interview except the employee is saying nothing, although he is listening intently to the manager. The manager is becoming concerned over the monologue but otherwise feels confident that everything is going smoothly and according to the book.

The manager decides to stop talking and asks the employee to share his views on the fairness and accuracy of the appraisal as well as his views about how the process is working out between the two of them. The employee, by no means a timid fellow, makes the following open, honest, authentic statements:

> I think your comments were accurate and that you prepared them so that I could clearly follow you. But, you know, I want to tell you something, Bob. I really don't care what you think about me or what I think about me or what the other guys think about me. I like my job okay. What I care about is what God thinks of me. So the performance review thing is just a ritual that goes along with your job, and it really doesn't bother me.

The manager does not know what to make of these statements because the employee has never shown any signs of such religious fervor. He has never talked about religion at work and has never used casual conversations around the coffee machine, water cooler, or cafeteria to proselytize employees into joining any religious cults. The manager is dumbfounded, has no riposte, and goes on with the remaining moments allocated to the appraisal to cover a few minor points. The employee remains affable but silent. The manager terminates the interview and quizzically turns over in his own mind what happened. He wonders: is this employee for real?

The employee in this situation has concepts of judgment that supervene performance appraisal. In fact, the manager should have noted that the employee defined the appraisal interview situation as one where the employee felt he was being judged as a person ("what you think of *me*") rather than assessed as a job incumbent who turned in a particular performance in a job. It might have been possible to switch the appraisal into an evaluation of the work (impersonal) instead of the individual employee (personal), thereby taking the discussion out of the realm of "theology" and into tangible matters that could be discussed fruitfully.

It could be argued that very few employees ever make the theological argument as stated: few Americans are so fundamentalistic or "born again." Yet the truth is that many workers perceive appraisals as report cards in industry and do not take them seriously. Also, they may not all fear the wrath of God, and the biggest things in their lives may be watching football on TV, planning the next vacation, jogging, or myriad other nonjob activities.

The employee's "theological" objection can undermine the effectiveness of appraisals as much as can a manager's reluctance to play God. The objections are as difficult to uproot; in extreme cases, changing the employee's attitude may not be worth the effort. Even if the employee opposes performance appraisal on theological grounds, when pay increases are tied to demonstrated job results, the employee is likely to give performance appraisals at least some attention, particularly if he is not a good performer and feels he may receive lower rewards than he would like.

The best strategy for a manager to use or for an organization to endorse is to focus on the employee's overt behavior and how it appears to affect work results.

Performance appraisal has a serious organizational purpose. Certain managers and employees have serious religious beliefs. These beliefs need not be made incompatible with the theory and practice of performance appraisals if the latter are behaviorally oriented and do not attack individual employee dignity and pride.

To date, performance appraisals have not been directly challenged in court as being discriminatory on religious grounds. Indirectly, there have been court cases involving employees who have been disciplined for refusing to work on their religious holidays. Viewed another way, it may be argued that such employees were evaluated as not performing the way management wanted purely from the standpoint of accepting work schedules and thus were discharged for performance-based reasons. Such employees have typically been reinstated on the grounds that employers should make reasonable adjustments of the work schedule to accommodate employees. This topic and its ramifications, however, seem somewhat far afield of the issues involved in formal performance appraisal systems as we are considering them in this book. Hence, we do not dwell upon them further.

25

A constructive performance appraisal at a minimum requires the participants in it to have sufficient self-awareness and insight so that they can appreciate and learn from the appraisal interview and process.

To THIS POINT, a variety of comments have already been made on the dynamics of the appraisal process and the sensitivities of the manager and employee to what is going on in the appraisal interview. We have also discussed "theological" objections to appraisals and how they crop up. Are there so many potential barriers to the success of the process that we might conclude the fight is not worth the candle?

Picture a closed-minded manager and a noncommunicative subordinate sitting opposite one another at a table during an appraisal interview. What are the chances that this situation is going to be fulfilling for both the boss and the subordinate? How do inarticulate people, individuals with suppressed anger, or persons who do not know themselves (on either side of the table) perform in an appraisal interview? The answers to all these questions suggest how common and widespread are the phenomena we have been discussing.

A constructive performance appraisal requires at the

minimum that participants in it have sufficient self-awareness and insight so that they can appreciate and learn from the specific appraisal interview underway and the overall process itself. A superficial review of the subordinate's goals and accomplishments during the year as described by the manager with some selective listening on the manager's part describes the appraisal interview at its best in many work organizations today. The interview has the potential for in-depth communication by two people but it is not realized.

The development of self-awareness and insight is a topic that transcends the content of the performance appraisal workshop/seminar described earlier. To be sure, the workshop/seminar through the use of experiential learning methods, closed-circuit TV, and role playing may provide some self-education for the manager. But since the workshop/seminar is not offered to subordinates, it will do them no good. It would be naive to propose that the solution to the problem is to offer high-quality sensitivity training to everyone on the payroll and see to it that all employees have a successful experience with it.

A practical solution to the problem may be coaching of selected managers who show such a manifest lack of self-awareness and insight that they botch the appraisal. Sending them to carefully monitored self-education programs may occasionally help a manager. But it should be cautioned that too much confidence in training is not warranted. Therapy may be needed.

The manager and subordinate will not learn much from the appraisal unless they have "learned how to learn." The latter phrase may sound confusing. What it means is that in self-education and related areas of behavior change, people need to develop the capacity to analyze what is taking place in interpersonal relationships and to plan what they should do next on the basis of that analysis. They have learned how to analyze and learned how to use that analysis. This may sound like a mystical process or double-talk but it is not. It is simply a way of viewing how adults develop a capacity to deal with social situations and convert them into successful problem-solving experiences.

Inasmuch as many people in industry will probably never learn how to learn as well as they might, this limitation will have an important bearing upon the adequacy of performance appraisals in American industry. Many observers of the field have great enthusiasm for the process and confidence in the mechanics of MBO and other systems. They seem not to realize how human imperfections and fallibility confound the process. Since there will always be imperfect and blocked people trying to implement the appraisal process, we will always have problems in the administration and follow-up of appraisals. We see no practical solution to this widespread problem.

26

The world's greatest experts on the employee's performance are the employee and the boss—not Sigmund Freud, Douglas McGregor, Abraham Maslow, the federal government, or the HR/PMD.

Recognizing the imperfections of the appraisal process and shortcomings of the boss and subordinate in carrying it out, the manager may think that by following the advice of experts in the field or experts on plumbing the human psyche, he can become more proficient as an appraiser of the work of a particular employee. This is not likely to be the case. The greatest experts on a particular employee's performance are the person doing the work and the person supervising the conduct of that work. Therefore, it is the employee and the boss—not Freud, McGregor, Maslow, the federal government, or the HR/PMD—who possess knowledge of the relevant facts of a case to the extent that even if these experts were present in a particular performance appraisal interview they could not help very much.

We are not trying to belittle the contributions of leading experts in human behavior and management to our understanding of the appraisal process in companies and agencies in a general and theoretical way. Appraisal has a heritage in theory and practice which should not be ignored, least of all by systems designers. The distilled knowledge of the past about the appraisal process and how such knowledge helps us understand the way in which appraisals should be carried out is very valuable. But the knowledge never goes far enough to pinpoint the job content in the job description of a particular employee in a specific organization for a specific year's performance which is being appraised. It is ludicrous to think that it should.

The HR/PMD in many organizations will have a file of up-to-date job descriptions and will retain the employee records, including a certain number of performance appraisals. Yet the HR/PMD will have less specific job performance knowledge than the manager or subordinate. As we noted earlier in the book, the HR/PMD should audit the effectiveness of the appraisal process in the company or agency. The HR/PMD is, however, always one step removed from the process and performance appraisal interview itself. Naturally, the HR/PMD cannot keep track of the myriad day-to-day informal contacts and appraisals of managers and subordinates. This removal from the scene places the HR/PMD at a disadvantage in registering first-hand observations and offering expert advice on performance problems. On the other hand, removal from the scene is appropriate staff conduct and fitting for the role of being observer and monitor of the overall performance appraisal system. Through the review of submitted appraisals the HR/PMD can bridge the pure staff role while keeping generally acquainted with how performance appraisals are being conducted. Also, upon request, a knowledgeable person from the HR/PMD may act as a third-party facilitator in some appraisal interviews where both the manager and subordinate feel the outsider might clarify and help the process.

The federal government normally takes no interest in job evaluation, employee selection, and performance appraisals unless there is litigation by individuals or the U.S. Department of Labor and trials before a court of law. The long arm of the government is not likely to offer much help and expertise on how the manager and subordinate should conduct themselves in evaluating how the employee met or failed to meet his job goals and duties and what type of developmental actions should ensue. Courts might look at the relative subjectivity or objectivity of the individual appraisal or the general system and its administrative consistency. But the appraisal task itself is uniquely left to the boss/subordinate set or pair.

We see once again that the role of the manager is critical in the process and that outside resources can be helpful and provide only general guidance.

27

Gamesmanship, rituals, and superficiality in
handling the appraisal need to be understood,
and methods for coping with them utilized.

The performance appraisal can become a psychological
jousting ring and offer a setting in which all kinds of rituals
and interpersonal games can be acted out.[8] Games may sound
like fun but they amount to chicanery and can become extremely befuddling as well as downright nasty and punitive.
When it appears that the jousting ring may result in the
manager's getting lanced, he may decide to defend himself by
keeping the appraisal innocuous and superficial or, if he is
hearty, draw upon an armamentarium of tools that will enable
him to take the offensive and ream the employee.

The key to the manager's taking a leading but not offen-
sively overbearing role in the appraisal is found in being
prepared and planning as much as possible how the interview
will proceed. The subordinate should be encouraged to par-
ticipate in the interview and should be given every opportunity
to communicate his perceptions of his performance in the
period under review. These considerations lead to spelling out

the elements of the best processes for actually administering an appraisal.

We summarize next the preparatory aspects of the performance review situation from the standpoint of the appraiser. First, he should ask himself a number of different questions. (Let us assume he is using the form from Figure 4.1.) How have I determined that the responsibilities and duties on the form adequately describe the job that the employee is actually performing? What have I done from day to day and in formal sessions with the employee so that he knows what his specific position responsibilities are? What have I done to make certain that the employee knows the quality and quantity of work expected of him? What measures have I taken to be certain that the performance incidents, trends, and on-the-job behavior cover the entire period since the past review and constitute a representative sample? What methods and techniques were used by the employee to carry out his specific assignments? What have I done to evaluate the strong and weak points and to avoid evaluating all aspects of the employee's work as average? What have I done as a manager to help carry out plans for improving the performance of the employee that were made at the last performance appraisal interview? What preparations have I made to answer questions about salary increases should these questions come up, even though discussion of salary is not the purpose of the interview? What circumstances exist that are beyond the employee's control and are affecting his performance? Does the employee show aptitudes and interests that indicate he may be more suitably placed in another position or line of work? What measures have I taken to make sure that this performance review represents the best unprejudiced estimate of the employee's typical performance in the period covered? Why has the employee performed at the level that he has for the period covered?

The manager who has asked himself such questions probably is as well prepared as he can be to conduct a performance appraisal. His next task is to conduct the appraisal interview itself, and this can put him on the top of the horse with a jousting stick or into an encounter that minimizes games, defensive behavior, counterjousts, and belligerence.

The appraiser should begin by creating an atmosphere that is conducive to effective two-way communication, which is, of course, much more easily said than done and is contingent upon all kinds of personal and organizational climate variables. Certainly, sufficient time should be set aside for the interview. The specific manner in which the atmosphere is established plays a very important part in the conduct and subsequent results of the performance appraisal interview. There is considerable debate over the proper way to create an atmosphere that will result in a performance appraisal that is successful from the standpoints of both the company or agency and the employee. It is hard to reduce the skills of climate building to anything resembling concrete guidelines without sounding simplistic and slick, but a few general remarks should prove helpful. At the outset, however, the employee should know clearly why he is there. In other words, the performance appraisal interview should begin with a statement of its purpose.

The appraiser should be capable of stating his observations clearly. Obviously, managers differ in the quality of their articulation. We have consistently argued that it is best to emphasize the performance of work rather than the traits of the individual employee in order to focus attention on specific objectives in the work situation and performance standards rather than elusive and subjective traits. Such an approach avoids name calling through the use of either emotionally loaded or emotionally interpreted adjectives. The approach requires training in the use of nonevaluative feedback.

The interview should then proceed to deal with the goals and accomplishments of the employee; these should be discussed as candidly and openly as possible. Finally, the interview should close with a summary to set up a plan for improvement with agreed-upon preliminary objectives, standards, and target dates for their accomplishment. If an MBO approach is being used, the interview itself probably will drift naturally into work planning for the next year and be followed up by subsequent discussions that winnow down into concrete objectives.

In the course of the interview, any number of topics may come up about which it is difficult to provide general guidance. In fact, it is the wide variety of topics, personalities, reactions, and organizational settings in which performance appraisals take place that complicates our discussion of the actual performance appraisal interview in more specific terms.

In any event, after the interview has been completed, the manager should reflect upon what took place in process and content, and upon what was accomplished. He may do this by asking himself a number of questions such as the following. Specifically, what was accomplished during the performance appraisal interview? Were the planned objectives of the interview met? What new items of information were brought up in the course of the interview that had not been previously considered? What can be done to assist the employee in developing himself on the job? To what extent was the employee willing to engage in self-appraisal? In what areas were there disagreements, and what has been planned to be done about these areas of disagreement? What can I do in the period between the present and the next performance review to assist the employee in attaining organizational objectives and meeting performance standards? What can be done to improve communications between me and the employee so that there is steady growth in both of us in relating to one another and accomplishing personal and organizational goals?

28

The "sandwich" technique and canned approaches to the appraisal interview divert attention from where it belongs in guiding one's behavior for an effective appraisal session.

In providing guidance for the manager on how to handle himself in the jousting ring we glossed over specific advice on techniques that can be used in the interview. This was a deliberate omission because we wanted to single out the subject for special attention as a separate guideline. It deserves special attention because so much of the advice given to managers on the appraisal process has been half-baked.

Consider the "sandwich" technique. Someone whose name is lost in history coined this phrase to mean that, in discussing an employee's performance with him, the manager should start with a positive statement, insert a negative one, go back to a positive one, then insert again a negative one, and so on, until the manager runs out of comments. The idea is to alternate the good and bad news about performance with verbal salami. Whether the technique is to be recommended universally is dubious. Whether it is best to begin an appraisal interview with positive comments rather than negative is not known. But praise should be used cautiously since it is judgmental and can cause uneasiness.

We actually know very little about how to give negative and positive feedback, although the former may be more of a problem than the latter. Perhaps it is best to give positive feedback in as highly specific a manner as possible to avoid conveying the impression to the employee that the totality of his performance was perfect and that he can walk on water. Everyone is likely to need improvement in some areas. On the other hand, negative feedback should probably be presented in as nonevaluative a manner as possible. Three to five work behaviors that are not up to par should be concentrated on and augmented with joint problem-solving discussions and short-term follow-up for the purpose of monitoring progress.

It would be very helpful if we could draw up a global list of the techniques that make for a successful appraisal interview and describe how they can be learned. The result would be a wealth of practical guidance that the manager can seize upon and use. We do not know how to specify the key points on such a checklist of guidance because the dynamics of the interview are truly as hard to capture as a bucket of steam.

There are books and courses on interviewing that can be helpful.[9] But after reading and attending to them the manager still may not know whether direct questions should be more numerous than indirect questions, whether the manager should level with an employee quickly or only after determining whether he can take it, what body language signifies, how much small talk there should be, how much humor to inject, and so on, endlessly. We despair of coming up with a cookbook of dos and don'ts for the appraisal interview, and the wise manager would not expect to find such a definitive list. A great deal in every performance appraisal interview hinges on idiosyncratic elements that are operating among the people involved, the time, and the place. This is why managers best learn interviewing techniques through skill practice, closed-circuit TV, case analysis, and similar methods of instruction.

We must fall back upon some points made earlier in the book and restate them in summary next.

We cannot rely on the mechanical application of techniques in any appraisal because the situation is dynamic. The manager and employee should be open, honest, authentic, and confronting—in short, sensitive to each other. They should approach the interview in a problem-solving, developmental frame of mind and have no axes to grind. They should be learning how to learn while interacting with one another and feel free to draw upon those techniques of human communication that seem appropriate to the occasion as it evolves.

29

MBO is far from perfect yet it is the best tool available for performance appraisal and reaching decisions on changes in pay.

MBO HAS BEEN MENTIONED SEVERAL TIMES in this book both directly and obliquely. It is far superior to any other method of performance appraisal and may be viewed as a system of management more than an appraisal method. Yet MBO has failed to work out in numerous organizations, perhaps because of misapplication. Probably in these cases it went through the stages that various management fads seem to follow:

- Excitement
- Confusion
- Disillusionment
- Search for the guilty
- Punishment of the innocent
- Rewards to the noninvolved

For managers, professional, and technical employees MBO seems nevertheless to have greater promise than any other approach in use today for providing a meaningful and successful performance review. The day may come when MBO is replaced by a better approach. Some people think that BARS (behaviorally anchored rating scales) are superior to MBO and represent the wave of the future. We doubt this and discuss BARS later in the book under guideline 38. We believe that MBO is far from perfect but that it is the best tool available for performance appraisals and reaching decisions on changes in pay.

MBO is built around the development-control concepts emphasized in this book and has the potential for avoiding the judgmental nature of the performance rating in which the boss is placed in the Godlike position of appraising the worth of a fellow man. The emphasis in management theory in recent years upon the manager as a leader who strives to help his subordinates achieve both their own and the work organization's objectives obviously is inconsistent with the role of the manager as a judge.

Under MBO the subordinate establishes short-term (usually defined to mean annual) performance goals for himself. The manager, who retains veto power on goals, assists the employee only after the subordinate has done a great deal of thinking about his job, made a careful assessment of his own strengths and weaknesses, and formulated some specific plans to accomplish his goals. The manager, in effect, helps the employee relate his self-appraisal, his "targets," so to speak, and his plans for the ensuing period to the realities of the organization. MBO properly installed begins as an extremely participative process. For clerical and office employees the MBO can be suitably tailored to emphasize performance standards on repetitive and routine work. (The mechanics of how to apply relevant and useful performance standards in these situations is beyond the scope of this book.[10])

Most of the prominent approaches to MBO are conceptually clear and amount simply to setting annual objectives and then measuring the results against the objectives twelve months later. The goals are set as objectively as possible and as quantitatively as possible so that the employee knows that at this point he has agreed to carry out some very specific and substantial work. The better MBO plans do not require a listing of detailed activities in which the employee intends to engage to implement his goals or a long laundry list of ancillary things to do. Instead, they express objectives in such a way that as time passes, data can be accumulated and related to particular objectives for the purpose of performance progress. Activity checks and reports on how activities turned out are not needed. Thus, from a performance appraisal standpoint, under MBO trait names are avoided, unguided judgment is channelized and reduced to a minimum, and participation and mutual goal setting are accommodated.

To this point we have described MBO at the level of the manager and subordinate. We do not mean to imply that MBO is solely a bottoms-up concept because it is best described as a participative top-down concept. To dwell on the bottoms-up aspect would imply that successively higher levels of management simply coordinate managerial work completed at lower levels, which would be a very passive characterization of management indeed! Figure 29.1 shows MBO as cascading down successive levels of management and, in the process, displays upward linkages as well, somewhat like a salmon leap.

In this perspective, MBO starts with corporate top management's carrying out its responsibilities for planning overall goals such as the annual profit plan or the equivalent. Managers at the divisional and departmental levels negotiate their responsibilities at successive levels of management, and the subordinate finally sets objectives in the way previously described as bottoms-up. The figure implies different levels of objectives and that the specificity of objectives increases the lower the organizational level of the employee.

Once the objectives are set, the employee and the manager discuss progress toward meeting the goals and modify them periodically as needed. They might do this quarterly or

FIGURE 29.1 The MBO cascade

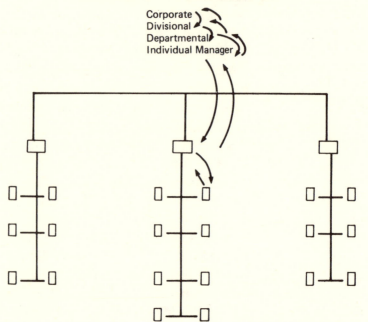

Source: Thomas H. Patten, Jr., *Pay: Employee Compensation and Incentive Plans* (New York: Free Press, 1977), p. 363.

monthly. Whenever needed, problem-solving meetings can take place between the two. In fact, anytime there has been a major change in the work situation that would justify changing an objective, the employee and the manager should meet and discuss a possible shift in direction.

The conventional period to which MBO applies is one year (either fiscal or calendar). MBO is, thus, short range but it can be wedded to long-range planning and other forms of strategic planning, which has been the case in its best applications.

The setting of objectives, negotiation of goals, implementation of activities necessary to fulfill goals, discussions of problems of goal attainment, shifting of direction, and eventual measurement of accomplishments (or shortfalls) typify the MBO cycle. Once the manager has made it a way of life and activated it as the way of running the job, the MBO system can be recycled and renewed indefinitely, assuming that it is properly maintained in the interim.

From what has been discussed, it should be clear that MBO has great potential for tying together top-down and bottoms-up goal setting in a participative way. MBO has the potential for letting employees know for sure what their performance is expected to be and informing managers how their work ties into the work of peers, superiors, and subordinates. Because MBO has such potential, it provides a clear basis for reaching decisions on changes in pay.

30

Managers and employees need training on MBO
as an overall system, on techniques for goal
setting, and skill practice in problem solving.

I<small>N THE DISCUSSIONS ABOVE</small> of the workshop/seminars on performance appraisals we mentioned the desired content of
training programs on appraisals. Part of that discussion
treated MBO in a general way.

If managers or employees are expected to change their
behavior and start functioning within an MBO framework,
they must be acquainted with MBO conceptually and techni-
cally. The contemporary manager who lacks goals or feels
caught in a work system that is incongenial or ineffective will
normally seek clarification of what is expected of him and
guidance as to how he is supposed to run his job. In a way, it
may be said that he seeks both a sense of direction and a style
of operating as a manager. Dealing with these two matters
may be antecedent training to that provided on the MBO-
based performance appraisal system itself. Similarly, employees have to know enough about goal setting, establishing
measurement indices for goals, and problem solving so that

they can change their behavior and make certain it is compatible with the style of a manager who is operating in an MBO mode.

The failures of MBO as an overall administrative system in American business and the public sector have many causes but certainly one of them has been attempts to implement MBO with little or no training, or with improper training. The result of this imposition of MBO on a manager is misapplication of a sound concept that is therefore doomed from the start. The hardiness of MBO to survive through second- and third-generation attempts at installation says a great deal for the inherent soundness of the concept as well as for the persistent need among managers for an objective-setting and performance-appraisal system that is a natural part of the way in which they run their jobs.

Any manager who is asked to change from his present method of managing his job to MBO should insist on instruction on systematic MBO, a workshop or one-on-one coaching in goal-setting techniques, and a workshop that allows him to practice his problem-solving skills. The content of this training and design for these workshops are beyond the scope of this book but are well known in American management education circles.[11]

31

The most advanced concepts of MBO emphasize simplicity and focus upon planning and controlling the fulfillment of assigned work; hence, MBO is a natural for use in the appraisal of performance, both for individual managers and employees and managerial teams.

PERHAPS ONE OF THE REASONS why MBO training has failed when given to managers in the past was that it was too elaborate and confusing and its compatibility with planning and control concepts was not obvious. Often, managers who had no prior management education to use as a foundation were unprepared for it. Paradoxically, the most advanced concepts of MBO emphasize simplicity and focus upon planning and controlling the fulfillment of assigned work. Figure 31.1 shows how simple an MBO-based performance appraisal form can be.

MBO may be regarded as a natural tool for use in the appraisal of individual managers and employees and managerial teams. The reason for this is that when MBO is properly applied, it is not something that is extra and above the way the manager runs his job but an explicit part of the job and its tasks, duties, and responsibilities. MBO is inherent in the natural manager-employee relationship. MBO focuses upon

FIGURE 31.1 Example of a type of MBO performance appraisal plan.

PERFORMANCE OBJECTIVES

Position: T. J. Logan, General Sales and Marketing Manager, Kahala Products Division

Specific Objectives for the Year 1983	Results Obtained and Explanations
1. To achieve the sales growth of 14% to $9 million, as set out in detail in the sales budget (Reference PX 13, dated October 1, 1982). These sales to be achieved within the expense budget stipulated.	1.
2. To complete preparations for the launching of product X by April 1, 1983.	2.
3. To text market product Y in New England district during August–September 1983 and recommend further action by October 1, 1983.	3.
4. To insure that forward market analyses are carried out covering the Z product range and possible developments for that range; report to the Product Development Committee by July 1, 1983. Recommending lines for R&D effort on this range.	4.
5. Improve the speed of order analysis to achieve daily order summarizes by product group by March 1, 1983. Develop follow-up procedures to investigate variation in intake by product group.	5.
6. Draw up organization and manning proposals by October 6, 1983, to separate the sales organization of Z product range by July 1, 1984.	6.

Source: Thomas H. Patten, Jr., *Pay: Employee Compensation and Incentive Plans* (New York: Free Press, 1977), p. 364.

these performance variables that are inherent in the actual work of the manager and employee and in the team of people whose individual performances are enhanced when they interface effectively.

MBO is a tool that is inextricably connected with team building so that the work commitment of team members can be increased and their desire to excel in performance can be inspired. Top management will usually hope for extraordinary accomplishment across the board but will probably settle for less as long as the mission or missions of the business or agency are accomplished. We often find that mission accomplishment will not take place unless individuals are interfacing effectively as teams and are sufficiently energetic to put forth the effort and extended commitment needed for results.

We have already seen that MBO may be viewed as either an overall management system or a sound method for structuring the performance appraisal process. There is a middle ground between these two polar concepts of MBO; this is found when we consider MBO as a planning and control process in much the same way as many MBO experts have done.

MBO as a managerial tool came into existence when it was found that a lack of planning and control usually meant extensive and disruptive organizational and management problems that, in turn, required a great deal of managerial time, energy, and attention for correction. As an alternative, MBO appeared to be a disciplined way of managing that involved a rational cycle of planning and controlling.[12] It had the potential for getting a handle on performance accountability.

MBO becomes a disciplined way of operating and means for implementing performance accountability only when managers have been trained to see these aspects of it and learned how to manage using MBO rather than some flakey alternative such as fire fighting immediate problems, pleasing the boss, reading the organization's political weathervane and then taking action, avoiding sacred cows and boat rocking, and the like.

32

MBO works best when managers in the head shed have a clear sense of mission and mission statements into which lower-level managers can plug their performance objectives.

A SUCCESSFUL INSTALLATION of MBO requires written mission statements that are prepared by the head shed, that is, the people at the highest levels of top management, such as the chief executive officer and chief operating officer and their immediate subordinates. (In the public sector, officials at analogous levels in the executive branch or legislative bodies and their leaders must define the mission and create what are essentially mission statements.)

Mission statements translate longer-range plans into shorter-range kinds of objectives that are suitable for fashioning into MBO performance appraisal goal items. Mission statements are analogous to an umbrella that covers the people under it. Mission statements allow the synchronization of human effort and help managers and employees think ahead, to set objectives that are challenging and meaningful for the next year rather than merely repeating what they did during the year past. Mission statements provide the coherence in which top-down and bottoms-up goal setting appear sensible and compatible.

The purpose of the mission statement is to link and give direction downward in the company or agency while allowing ample freedom for subordinates to draft their own objectives within these boundaries. Mission statements are very brief and when digested can be almost telegraphic in their message. They are usually written in such a way that persons not employed by the company or agency to which the mission applies have trouble understanding them. The statements are drafted in such a way that managers and employees inside the organization can understand them and appreciate that they carry clear overtones of being authoritative mandates for action.

Mission statements should be revised by the head shed annually or as often as needed when the direction of the organization is going to be changed.

The terminology of "mission" and "objective" may sound confusing and need reviewing for the manager. A mission statement applies to many managers, sets broad direction, is difficult to measure, and is done in a joint session involving groups or teams of people at the pinnacle of top management. An objective or goal (synonymous terms as we have used them) has applicability to an individual manager or employee, or singular accountability. It specifies end results. It is relatively easy to measure progress toward an objective anytime such measurement is desired. It is developed by a pair consisting of a manager and a subordinate rather than in a meeting at which a large number of people are present. The linkage between the mission as mandated and the objectives as specified (and translated into behavior on the job) creates the legitimacy of performance appraisal. In other words, managers will know what to plug into if there are mission statements; otherwise goal-oriented behavior becomes a guessing game.

33

MBO is properly installed when it is voluntarily accepted in an organization and not forced down the organization from top management—with or without vaseline!

MBO CAN BE APPLIED SUCCESSFULLY to an organization that has sufficient autonomy and personnel, budgetary, and policy integrity such that it can operate relatively free from imposition of an excessive number of external constraints. In many companies or agencies budget responsibility is delegated to managers who are held accountable for work results based upon their management of office space, material resources, financial resources, and human resources. Managers are expected to perform so that goals are attained by the organization.

An organization, if it satisfies the criteria specified above, could be a company of any size, a plant in a large company, a large department in a plant, an agency of any size, a state university system, a campus of a state university system, a hospital, and so on. Many organizations are, in other words, subsystems in larger systems. It is not size or type which satisfies our definition of organization, but personnel, budgetary, and policy integrity.

Managers in organizations will find MBO a powerful and useful tool for the disciplined practice of managerial work if it is properly installed. Too often MBO is installed top-down in a dictatorial manner with little or no accompanying training. The abrasiveness of the imposition hurts, and vaseline in the form of memoranda and pep talks on how MBO will be a panacea of performance problems does little to alleviate the pain.

MBO as a system should be installed from the top of the organization down, complete with mission statements. Paradoxically, the installation should have a voluntary aspect to it. Few managers are likely to resist a useful planning and control system, although some might. Rather than force those managers to accept MBO, it is preferable to act opportunistically and follow the path of least resistance in the installation. Successful application of the MBO system by those who use it voluntarily will probably result in a certain amount of boasting. The resulting peer pressure may coax the reluctant manager into giving MBO a trial. With proper installation, success stories about how MBO worked out as a way of running the job and conducting performance appraisals may then become individual fires in an organization and eventually coalesce. The result will be a great conflagration, which in terms of the end result will amount to organizational installation of MBO. On the other hand, if MBO does not catch fire, it is preferable to let it function where it is wanted rather than force it on the reluctant manager through application of pressure from the head shed.

Voluntarism versus compulsion is often an issue in the installation of any system in management. We argue that managers should make a choice about what works for them in obtaining adequate performance from their subordinates. If, for example, a manager appears to be obtaining excellent results at work, there is no reason to force him (with or without vaseline) to accept a new and (for him) untried system. Naturally, top management must have evidence that the manager is truly effective and that they are not being duped. In addition, the HR/PMD needs to audit its records to verify that a manager's hesitancy to adopt MBO is not deleterious to the work organization.

A manager may actually be working in an MBO mode already and not realize it. To force such a person to stop what he is doing that makes him successful as a manager so that he will accept an organizationally endorsed version of MBO seems irrational and potentially capable of turning an excellent, motivated manager into a mediocre, unhappy one!

34

MBO-based performance appraisal systems must
be synchronized with budgetary realities and
coordinated with all relevant corporate public
policy goals.

MANAGERS WHO HAVE RESPONSIBILITIES for goal attainment
also have resources (financial, material, and human) made
available to them so that they can attain their goals. Financial
control systems in companies and agencies are usually put well
in place long before much attention is paid to other systems
created by staffs. An employee performance review system is
thus usually a latecomer compared to the installation of, for
example, a financial accounting system. It is for this reason
that we observe organizations apparently going off in several
different directions at once. The budget formalization process,
for illustration, might proceed quite independently of the
MBO system and the basis for performance appraisals. The
annual profit plan may be set by very high levels of management and then handed down to the lower managers for implementation without regard to the implications it may have
for the managers who have already set goals in their own areas
with their own people. The mission statement may be out of

date or ignored by top management because its attention is overly focussed on some current and urgent corporate drive.

MBO-based performance appraisal systems do not have much of a chance for successful operation when they are not synchronized with budgetary realities and coordinated with relevant corporate public policy goals. For example, if a manager and his subordinates plan their goals very conscientiously and start working toward them only to be told that their salary budget is going to be cut by 15 percent and that they are expected to absorb certain operations which were hitherto performed by another department, managers are likely to become cynical about the priority that the organization places on MBO-based performance appraisals. They will realize that they have been asked to perform work for which resources have not been allocated. Those programs and efforts that *are* emphasized will get their attention in the future, and work planning will subsequently be opportunistic. MBO will be looked upon as a pet paper program of the HR/PMD or some top executive who happens to like it and therefore as something not to be taken seriously. Top management's actions will be interpreted to mean that managers are not supposed to manage but to follow orders that shift like the wind.

It is not difficult for a manager to continue to manage as he has in the past, closely observe the movements of the corporate weathervane, prepare paper MBO goals and make them look meaningful, and survive on the organization's payroll. Performance then becomes successful survival—even obtaining handsome pay adjustments—in a turbulent environment. Performance has little or nothing to do with obtaining results in a rational business framework.

Performance appraisal systems, as we have seen repeatedly, stand or fall on how they are used by the manager. The manager who cannot reconcile budgetary and other business policy goals with the narrower performance appraisal system under his control may take the easy way out: sit back, don't worry about performance, and wait till the signals change. Such a manager becomes a passive player but an ace survivor.

35

MBO can be used both in reviewing the
performance of individuals and natural intact
work teams—and should be used for both
whenever feasible.

Managers normally think of performance appraisal as a
one-on-one process consisting at its core of an interview between themselves and a subordinate for determining how well
the employee is doing on the job and how he can improve. As a
result of the process, it is hoped that the goals of the boss,
subordinate, and employing organization will be satisfied.
Team MBO enters in where individual goal setting leaves off.

If traditional one-on-one MBO is working well, the manager and subordinate may be collaborating and communicating very clearly. But several problems may crop up if we
consider how the manager may be interacting with other subordinates.

In many companies and agencies it is important to have effective teamwork among a group of managers or a group of
subordinates. The work cannot be done properly unless people
extend themselves to one another and do not take the nar-
rowest possible view of their own duties. It is not sufficient in
these situations that subordinates communicate with peers on

their own level and that goal setting is left up to one-on-one relations with the organizational superior. The group of employees or subordinates must be looked upon as a team that needs to be brought together. Goals now should be set by manager-subordinate pairs, and also by teams.

In moving toward team MBO and performance appraisals, after one-on-one goal setting has taken place, the persons involved in the team effort meet to discuss one another's goals under the direction of the manager so that they may decide how the goals of each other can best be met while synergistically meeting the organizational unit's overall goals. This discussion may involve considerable renegotiation of goals, the elimination of duplication and overlap, and the identification of ways in which all the employees involved can help each other.

The basic superior-subordinate relationship in the company or agency is in no way undermined in this concept of team goal setting. Lines of responsibility, authority, and accountability remain clear; the main change is that a new dimension has been added that recognizes the reality of the need for intrateam cooperation. Team MBO also opens the door for an approach to individual pay and team pay as well as for individual and team goal setting.

As yet very few organizations in the United States have developed methods of team MBO and for determining team compensation as an extra beyond individual pay. The major exception to this generalization is the executive bonus plans in corporations which are based upon supplementing the base pay of managers (primarily) in a formularized way based upon the overall profit performance of the corporation. Bonus plans often fail to stimulate managerial performance because they are overly formularized and do not allow enough leeway for the individual's contribution to profitability to shine through. It is possible, however, to design bonus plans so that greater room is provided for team MBO while individual MBO can be properly recognized. Peer ratings would appear to have great value in appraising the team efforts of an individual.

The wise manager recognizes the need to obtain individual performance and team performance. He knows how to function in the process of administering performance appraisals for individuals in the domain of their own job descriptions. He needs to learn how to factor in the extent the individual has been an effective team member and to reward him for effective teamwork. In order to do this the manager needs to know how to deal with groups and to encourage them to work together so that goal overlaps and duplication are avoided. This takes interpersonal skill but does not seem to require any radically different knowledge about MBO performance appraisal systems than has already been described.

36

For it to work, MBO knowledge must be accompanied by knowledge and skill practice in time management; otherwise managers may focus on the trivial and/or delegable aspects of their work and not complete crucial assignments.

T HE RESISTANCES of many managers to getting solidly behind a performance appraisal system and making it work for them have been mentioned many times. A common source of resistance is that managers do not have the time to involve themselves in appraisals, particularly if they require the amount of time and attention that MBO entails for other purposes.

There is an obvious but often neglected connection between MBO and time management and interpersonal communications. It seems that when an adequate MBO system is installed and functioning properly, many time-management and interpersonal communications problems seem to go away. While this does not sound like a profound observation, it nevertheless reflects the experience of many managers who feel squeezed for time and cannot pinpoint the cause of the pressure.

The key to getting straightened out may rest in obtaining

knowledge and skill practice in the management of their time, which may be regarded, from a different vantage point, as solving planning and control problems. Time is truly the scarcest resource for managers, and unless it is properly managed, nothing else can be managed, including performance appraisals.

An effective manager knows how to manage by getting results and how to delegate work to subordinates. Managers who have time-management problems attributable to inadequate skill in delegation can start to get a handle on their problems if they adher to the following maxim in dealing with subordinates: "Don't bring me your problems; bring me your solutions." A manager who is experiencing reverse delegation might very well apply the maxim to subordinates who are not completing their work properly and are coming to the boss permaturely to ask him to do their work for them. The manager should work with such subordinates to help them develop the skills, knowledge, attitudes, and behavior so that they can work in the future in a Theory Y mode with the boss. Put another way, for a manager to obtain control over his time so that he can plan and implement the tasks that are appropriate for his organizational level, he must carefully control the impositions on his time caused by subordinates who seek his guidance in unreasonable and overly large doses.

The philosophy of "don't bring me your problems; bring me your solutions" is very consistent with the type of MBO-based performance appraisal system that we have set forth in this book. Through proper goal setting and work planning the subordinate and manager should have developed a track on which to run. Through occasional freewheeling in problem solving by the boss and subordinate working one on one (or in a team), clear directions in assignments can be set and reverse delegation controlled. A manager cannot, however, move into being an effective delegator until his subordinates are adequately trained to handle all the requirements of the delegated job. It is the manager's responsibility to provide or have provided to the employee the training a subordinate needs to satisfy acceptable standards of job performance.

Managers who concentrate their energies on completing crucial assignments rather than the trivial and/or delegable activities and work are performing the job they are paid to fulfill. Moreover, managers who work at the appropriate level are likely to obtain very significant results from their work while those who spend their time on work that should be performed by their subordinates will have far fewer results, become overworked, and probably be viewed as less effective managers.

37

There is no such thing as "instant MBO"; hence, a trial period of three to five years is required to make the transistion to a fairly smooth MBO-based performance appraisal system.

TIME AFFECTS MBO-BASED PERFORMANCE APPRAISAL SYSTEMS in many ways. Top management in companies and agencies often wants to move from one performance appraisal system to another as rapidly as possible—like overnight! Everything we have discussed in this book suggests that "instant MBO" cannot be achieved. The design and preparation of the system, training of managers on how to use it, and auditing and follow-up cannot possibly be done in less than three years, except perhaps in very small organizations.

A serious misapplication in installing an appraisal system is to copy that of another organization and impatiently apply it in the hope that time will be saved. A performance appraisal system needs to be fashioned to fit, and while there is no need to reinvent the wheel, we cannot avoid certain reasonable time requirements to obtain a proper and comfortable fit.

Top managers who become enthusiasts of performance appraisal systems are often unwilling to wait three to five years for a system to be installed and to work out the kinks so that the desirable results are forthcoming. Their impatience leads to a waning of interest in the system and trying another before the first has had a chance to demonstrate its potential.

Managers become restless about results for many reasons, not the least of which is that they tend to think in terms of a fiscal or calendar year and of what can be done in that time to look good on paper. Longer-range planning exists, but a three to five year waiting period for maturation of an appraisal system seems inordinately long. Also, recognizing the realities of life in today's dynamic organizations, managers may not still be in their present jobs in three to five years time. They are likely to ask themselves: "Why should I spend my time and money for a human-resource management tool that won't have payoff while I'm here? What am I supposed to do about performance information between now and the time when the system matures? I simply can't wait to know for sure how well subordinate managers are doing. So go out and buy or improvise something that is practicable, even if it isn't the best."

The manager who administers performance appraisals may also feel impatient about system installation and improvement. The best course of action is to go slowly and work out the kinks of the system even though the progress will not be rapid. Care and understanding support are the watchwords, even though they may not be exciting ones to competitive managers who want instant results and evidence of their own accomplishments to show to the boss in the hope of obtaining more pay, a promotion, or some other reward.

38

Behaviorally anchored rating scales are a current fad that are thought by some to be improvements on MBO but do not offer the manager a viable alternative in performance appraisal.

BEHAVIORALLY ANCHORED RATING SCALES (which are known by the catchy acronym, BARS) have been given some attention in recent years because they do provide a way of grounding appraisals in objective reality and are a possible alternative to MBO. For the manager who does not like MBO or alleges that he cannot work within an MBO performance appraisal format, BARS may seem easier to use. A preferable solution would be training and coaching the manager to use MBO!

Broadly viewed, BARS are a contemporary version of the critical-incidents approach to performance appraisal, which we discussed earlier in the book and dismissed as of little concern to the practicing manager of today because virtually no companies and agencies have adopted critical-incidents performance appraisal systems. Those who do not know or care about history are doomed to repeat it, and BARS have arisen as an apparent innovation in performance rating scales but are really just a variation of critical incidents.

BARS are devices that display the spread of concrete behavior on a job from best to worst. Figure 38.1 displays how a scale might be developed for the one job dimension identified as meeting today's deadlines. A BARS for any particular job would consist of identifying a complete range of behaviors pertinent to that job and designing the relevant scales. If an organization had one hundred jobs and ten dimensions for each job, BARS construction would be a difficult and expensive task. But if it had one thousand jobs with ten dimensions, the costs, time , and effort involved would probably rule out adopting BARS. (These were about the same objections to the critical-incidents approach, and caused its demise.)

BARS, like MBO, can be defended in theory because they do focus on on-the-job behavior rather than on traits and could have value in defending a company or agency in a lawsuit as compared to graphic rating scales, which represent a subjective approach to evaluation. BARS can help enormously in channelizing judgments, although they are not perfect (nor, of course, is any appraisal method).

BARS are constructed to provide intervals on a scale that appear to be equal, although this may be more a figment of human imagination than a real distinction in psychological distance. BARS are tailor made to the job under consideration although they are not tailored to the specific objectives of *each job incumbent* for an annual period, as can be true with MBO. This is a major difference for the manager who seeks to wed planning and controlling the conduct of assigned work with its appraisal after elapsed time. BARS are too general for this purpose.

On the other hand, BARS could be used in an MBO mode (especially in jobs in the lower organizational levels) if the tasks in the job are sufficiently stable or routinized such that they will invariably lead to relatively invariant goals. Yet BARS are not project oriented, nor are they designed to integrate a particular work unit's goals with those of other work units.

FIGURE 38.1 Behaviorally anchored rating scale for a manager's meeting daily deadlines.

Could be expected never to be late in meeting deadlines, no matter how unusual the circumstances

Could be expected to meet deadlines comfortably by delegating the writing of an unusually high number of orders to two highly rated selling associates.

Could be expected always to get his associates' work schedules made out on time.

Could be expected to meet seasonal ordering deadlines within a reasonable length of time.

Could be expected to offer to do the orders at home after failing to get them out on the deadline day.

Could be expected to fail to schedule additional help to complete orders on time.

Could be expected to be late all the time on weekly buys for his department.

Could be expected to disregard due dates in ordering and run out of a major line in his department.

Could be expected to leave order forms in his desk drawer for several weeks even when they had been given to him by the buyer after calling his attention to short supplies and due dates for orders.

Source: John Campbell *et al., Managerial Behavior: Performance and Effectiveness* (New York: McGraw-Hill, 1970, p. 122.)

BARS do not represent another crusade in the search for the Holy Grail in performance evaluation because interest in them has been retarded owing to costs. For all but the wealthiest organizations that are willing to goldplate the budgets of the HR/PMD, we should not expect to see BARS made practicable.

39

All performance appraisal systems—including those founded on **MBO** concepts—can become obsolete, poorly administered, or susceptible to litigation; hence, they need to be reviewed as overall systems periodically by the HR/PMD and outsiders, as well as by managers.

THE MANAGER IS THE CENTRAL ACTOR in the performance appraisal drama, and a continuing campaign must be mounted to keep him a supporter and knowledgeable performer is sustaining the vitality of the system. From time to time managers should be asked about the system from their standpoint and how and where it could be improved. This would be an important step toward preventing obsolescence, inadequate administration, and possible lawsuits. Coupled with audits by the HR/PMD as discussed previously, the solicitation of suggestions from managers should go a long way toward system monitoring.

Outsiders can add importantly to the monitoring effort by providing both managers and the HR/PMD with yet another perspective. By "outsider," we mean either external or internal consultants who are removed from the performance appraisal system as either creators of it or administrators who work with it as one of their managerial tools. The comments that follow are geared to actions that managers should carry out with outside help to keep an MBO-based performance appraisal system vital.

First, as has already been discussed, every newly appointed manager should be provided with two to three days of training on the company's or agency's performance appraisal system, including the techniques for reducing goals to written measurable terms. Ideally, this training in concept and technique should be provided by an inside or outside consultant (or conceivably by a successful practicing line or staff manager who would be detailed to provide this kind of training). There should also be annual clinics or workshops for experienced managers on performance appraisal problems and on new ideas for improving the system, such as introducing the team dimension to appraisals.

Second, the outsiders should evaluate how the system is working in practice by spot-checks. Their unique perspective should be particularly helpful, particularly if they happen to be familiar with a broad range of practices in other companies or agencies. This effort should be a continuous one, and the goal should be to keep the program practicable given the changing environment and conditions of the world of work.

Third, the outsiders should work at every level of management to determine if the performance appraisal system is functioning everywhere in a synchronized manner. This would include reviewing the mission statements and all aspects of the MBO cascade. The outsiders would provide a logical feedback loop for all levels of management and for the HR/PMD so that the latter can make design changes where they are needed.

Fourth, the outsiders need to determine that every manager has job-content goals but also objectives that require him to have equal employment opportunity, employee development, occupational safety and health, and subordinate career-planning targets as well. Moreover, the "administrative skill" of every manager should be evaluated continually as a part of the performance appraisal so that both means and ends are studied. A part of this look at goals should also concentrate on whether the manager's goals are innovative. Every manager should have some creative goals to fulfill annually so that obsolescence does not slip in or the manager does not lapse into the cozy habit of applying last year's answers to this year's (and all future) problems.

What should be looked at in selecting an outsider to work with managers and the HR/PMD? This question is worth answering for the practicing manager because the woods are full of MBO and other consultants who profess to know all the ins and outs of the complex process of appraisal.

The best consultant is one who has had at least five years' experience in *all* phases of MBO, not merely its performance appraisal, compensation, or training aspects. He should have made at least one full-scale MBO installation and lived with it for a minimum of three years. He should be able to provide anyone who retains his services with specific examples of how each phase of MBO works, including the crucial aspect of MBO applied in performance appraisal. He should be able to provide references to prior clients with whom he has worked and should be open about his successes and failures. Everyone has an occasional bomb in his consultative work. He should be personally acceptable and on the same wavelength as the people with whom he is working in order to facilitate communication. He should be willing to stay with the client long enough to implement his efforts and surmount any significant problems that might arise. Yet he should not prolong the client's dependence on him. He should complete his work in a reasonable amount of time and leave managers in the system with adequate knowledge of the processes and adequate skill in using them without his assistance.

Outsiders who operate in the manner described can provide managers and the HR/PMD with the guidance they need to shape and steer the performance appraisal system.

40

When performance appraisal systems are linked
directly to pay determination decisions, special
design features are needed to help managers
obtain what they need in concepts and
techniques to manage adequately.

It is now time to return to the issue of two appraisals
(separate ones for development and for pay which were discussed in Chapter 5) since sufficient guidance has now been
provided in respect to the many issues in appraisal that had to
be analyzed before we were ready to talk about pay for performance itself.

Earlier in the book we suggested that separate performance
appraisal systems can be justified in smaller companies and
agencies and for those organizations that are newly experiencing the movement into formal performance appraisal. There is
economy and efficiency in gradually moving from a dual to a
single system. This move can be made when an organization
matures and has had considerable experience with performance appraisal systems for employee development and feels
ready for the ultimate in system integration.

Special design features are needed in single appraisal
systems to help managers obtain what they need by way of

concepts and techniques to manage properly.[13] The most important of these features is an MBO commitment. If we are to pay for performance, we must know what a manager's or employee's goals are in as clear a manner as possible and must have attempted to identify measures and indices of their attainment. We cannot design a graphic rating scale that will fulfill this purpose. BARS are a theoretical possibility but they have severe practical disadvantages. We might consider other possibilities also but are likely to come back to MBO.

Let's go out on a limb. In order to pay for performance our only hope is MBO! While this may seem like a strong and sweeping statement that places too much trust in a system that has frequently failed, the reader is invited to try to refute it by citing examples or experiences where a pay-for-performance system was based upon a different concept and different techniques and succeeded. To build the system on MBO by no means guarantees success; to build it without MBO is impossible. The limb may now be sawed off!

Once managers learn how to work within an MBO framework, they can use the goals in the MBO job content and the extras that go along with the job (equal opportunity objectives, administrative skills, employee development responsibilities, and the like) as items that can be weighed and quantified on a judgmental scale of importance. For example, we saw in Figure 31.1 how T. J. Logan's specific objectives for the year were quantified. Inasmuch as not all goals are on the same plane of importance, weights for their varying importance can be derived by the manager and subordinate in a joint session.

The MBO mode that allows weighting and joint goal setting must also be designed so that a true negotiatory spirit engages the manager and subordinate during the goal-setting interview. The potential always exists for the design to be corrupted into one where the boss nails down the goals, forces them on the subordinate, unilaterally determines the weights, and sends the employee on his way. The latter feels he has been placed in a ratchet, and that the screws will gradually be turned down on him. The feeling of entrapment can lead to resentment, demotivation, and a decision to seek employment elsewhere as soon as possible. Outsiders can review this type of performance appraisal system (as can the HR/PMD perhaps) to determine its dysfunctions and recommend design features so that the mode is made truly participative, a Theory *Y* style used for a Theory *Y* purpose.

The properly participative performance appraisal system is designed to allow the manager and subordinate jointly to set weighted goals (and change them if circumstances warrant) and to determine to what extent the goals have been achieved. Here again quantitative data are the most useful, although qualitative data are acceptable whenever quantitative data cannot be obtained. (It often happens that managers and subordinates who have trouble identifying means for measuring goal attainment quantitatively become in time and with experience capable of obtaining numerical measures of what was previously considered exclusively qualitative.)

From the data on goal attainment the manager can then move to a discussion of the proper amount of salary adjustment or supplemental compensation. The discussion may range over employee-development issues, career planning, the use of future job assignments for growth, and similar matters. In other words, when properly designed, a performance appraisal system in a company or agency whose managers have worked within its framework for three to five years can cater to *both* employee development *and* pay determination. The same system *can* serve both purposes and eliminate the need for a dual system, a serious problem in the administration of performance appraisal systems that could ultimately be solved in a practicable way.

41

Pay changes can be tied to MBO-based performance reviews in very subjective and very objective (almost mindlessly mechanical) ways; but in either case, in mature organizations pay must be tied in with performance appraisal.

THE SUBJECTIVE PERFORMANCE APPRAISAL, if based upon MBO, should be avoided and is indeed not necessary because the appraisal interview can be extremely goal-focussed within the job description. Why be subjective and open the door to prejudiced views? Pay adjustments that flow from subjective discussion and might result in employee disgruntlement encourage employees to think about redress—and protected groups to think in terms of class-action lawsuits.

The best approach for the manager who wants to move from a performance appraisal interview discussion into specifying what would be an appropriate pay adjustment is to stick to weighted, negotiated employee goals and the relevant quantitative data that apply to them. The author has described elsewhere the details of how an MBO performance plan, MBO performance report, an MBO accomplishments or results report, and a certain kind of merit increase conversion table can be used by the manager to link the appraisal to specific dollar amounts of merit money.[14] These forms are essentially derivatives 'of those in Figures 4.1 and 31.1. The merit increase conversion table and other mechanisms that have been developed by salary administrators over the years are popular devices for the manager's deriving within guidelines what an appropriate employee pay adjustment should be. Most salary administration books provide illustrations of these matters.

From a policy standpoint, the crucial consideration in American industry is *how* objective we want the manager to be in salary adjustment or bonus decisions. The growth of technique in compensation administration has been so vast in the past two decades that the issue is one of choice. We can select within the range of an extremely narrow technology on one end of the spectrum versus, on the other end, an alternative that allows the manager varying amounts of leeway in choosing an adjustment that allows the exercise of some judgment. We obviously do not want to remove all authority for granting an increase of a given size from the discretion of the manager. He should be able to decide within policy guidelines whether an increase should be 8 or 9 or 10 percent, and not be forced to move mechanically from the appraisal to one and only one dollar amount (such as 8 percent but no more or less) determined by a rigid salary schedule.

If the manager has no delegated authority to select an appropriate amount of pay increase, he may lose a certain amount of face and also lose one of the most useful motivational tools in the armamentarium of human-resource management. Every employee needs to be treated as an individual and recognition given to his unique situation as well as any extenuating circumstances that bear upon his performance. Too many mechanical controls can destroy the manager's flexibility in dangling the salary carrot. This is not to imply a belief in the universal appeal of money as a motivator, but it is silly to argue that it is not salient for most employees most of the time. How many employees will come to work on a Monday if told by the employer the previous Friday that there is plenty of work to do but no money to pay for it?

42

**The most impressive selling point for top
management about performance-based pay is
that it holds the potential for making work
rewards motivational, causing, as the case might
be, employees to work harder and/or smarter.**

Top management and lower management have been extremely concerned about motivation and productivity in America in recent years. For them, performance-based pay is a dream they would like to transform into a reality. They seek means to bring it about but often fail. There is a large school of thought consisting of keen observers who despair of the very idea. Some have nobly tried to implement the concept and failed after expenditures of time, money, and staff resources.

Within this backdrop of hopes and experiences, managers and HR/PMD specialists must exercise caution in improvising their own versions of performance-based pay. It is easier to conjoin the means for building a sound pay plan through job evaluation, salary surveys, and salary administration than it is to create and maintain a solid, effective performance appraisal system. Put another way, in the pay-for-performance conundrum, it is easier to fashion the pay aspects (which are mainly technical in nature) than the performance appraisal aspects (which are human problems). The solution rests in MBO-based systems that are developed and applied along the lines advocated in this book.

There is always a danger in overselling what a performance appraisal system can do for a company or agency and its managers at all levels. We have discussed how it can help employees work "harder" or "smarter" depending upon what their tasks require in terms of human effort—brawn or brains. Top management must endorse the concept of pay for performance, stay with it through prosperity and recession, and be patient for results. In acting in these ways, top management sends signals to lower levels of management and employees alike that they should settle in and work the kinks out of whatever performance appraisal and performance-based pay plan they choose as a starting point down what will probably be a fairly long road.

There is ample justification for a reasonable selling of the concepts of MBO-based performance appraisal systems and performance-based pay. Social-science research and the experience of pace-setting firms clearly point in these directions, but not without storm clouds, to be sure. Pay that is based philosophically on longevity (length of service or seniority) certainly has few champions these days in managerial circles. Are there any observers of today's American economic scene who see our problem of motivation and productivity being solved by using seniority as the sole criterion for pay adjustments?

43

Any top management that operates by the panic button and constantly shifts its attention from one problem to another depending upon perceived crises probably cannot and will not provide the stability and ambience for an effective performance appraisal system; hence, it should not bother to go through the exercise and charade!

A PERFORMANCE APPRAISAL SYSTEM does not grow well in a crisis-ridden, fire-fighting environment. The manager who wants to live in a more rational world of planning and control should either try to change the ambience where crises are chronic or leave it to seek greener pastures. We sometimes wonder if managements can live interminably in aggravation. Apparently some organizations have been born, have lived, and have died in a chronic crisis ambience.

The story about performance appraisal systems in such environments can be either a long one or a short one. It can be as long as the crises that punctuated the history of the system before its demise. It can be as short as finding out ultimately that the exercise to install the particular performance appraisal system was futile and that the props used to buck it up as it fell apart amounted to a sad charade. There is a lesson here for all levels of management: don't install a performance appraisal system unless you really want to give it a serious trial and intend to live by it!

Fortunately, most American companies and agencies sooner or later decide to try various types of management and corporate planning and control systems. In fact, "corporate strategy" has become a new buzz-word in management of the 1980s, which signifies that any organization should start with strategy before it flails around attempting to produce products or sell services. Because planning should precede action, we see an increasing number of companies and agencies that are amenable to the installation of performance appraisal systems. They then hope that managers can somehow bring it off and use it to implement corporate strategy.

44

Managers need to know the evolving legal principles about performance appraisals and to base all their employee-relations actions on defensible objective data.

Managers cannot be converted into attorneys, nor should they be. But they need to know the general principles that evolve about the conduct of employee appraisals so that if the appraisals should be challenged, they can stand up under legal scrutiny. Primarily, managers have to be trained, retrained, informed, and admonished to base all their dealings with employees on objective data as much as possible. Above all, personnel transactions should be untainted by prejudice and should reflect consistency in administration with departures only when they may be justified by mitigating circumstances.

Court cases on employee selection and on employment decisions made by managers that involve any type of paper-and-pencil test or instrument (such as a performance appraisal form) have proliferated since 1970 and will undoubtedly grow in the 1980s. The HR/PMD has the responsibility for keeping abreast of these developments in case law and normally works with corporate or agency counsel or outside attorneys to stay current. Managers should not attempt to keep up with case law or attempt to become "sea lawyers." The duty of the HR/PMD is to keep managers informed about the changing legal guidelines that apply to human-resource decisions so that managers understand the constraints under which they work and will make lawful personnel transactions.

We cannot detail the legal boundaries for performance appraisal systems and their administration here. But they can be sketched in a broad way, recognizing that the law is never static but is constantly evolving.

The Uniform Guidelines on Employee Selection Procedures issued in 1978 cover tests and other selection procedures that are used as a basis for any employment decision. This would include hiring, firing, promotion, demotion, retention, or almost any personnel decision affecting the employment status of an employee. Clearly then, a performance appraisal system with its component instruments represents a test that needs to be validated. Validity in job performance is difficult to measure but the more the appraisal process is formalized, reduced in detail to written form, and objective in what it seeks to measure, the better are the circumstances for approaching a measure of validity. The system should be job related and the appraisal should be based upon duties and responsibilities that are derived from a job analysis or stated in an up-to-date job description. Raw, unguided, subjective judgment about job performance should not be a part of the appraisal. Managers should be trained to administer the system. Methods of appraisal that concentrate on job assignments directly, such as MBO, have the greatest potential for yielding defensible data and for demonstrating that an attempt is being made in good faith to appraise and measure performance.

While MBO oversees the design, administration, and use of performance appraisal, the existing tenets of case law have developed from appraisal efforts devoid of these integrating influences. No single laundry list of appraisal system characteristics that would unquestionably render an appraisal system lawful has yet been developed. One can, however, gain insight into the areas that have received judicial scrutiny. Such areas of concern are presented here not as a legal checklist but rather as an interrelated pattern of elements to strive for:

- Clear performance criteria are developed from job analyses or job descriptions. There is avoidance of trait-oriented terms, and stress is placed on behavior-oriented performance dimensions.
- Appraisal system reliability and validity information is documented—before it is challenged.
- The objectives and use of the performance appraisal information are clearly communicated to those being evaluated.
- Evaluators are given formal training with written instructions.
- Measures have been taken to avoid situations where a single (and possibly biased) evaluator has sole control over the appraisal process. The use of multiple evaluators is best where it is possible.
- Employees are made aware of the performance standards they are being expected to achieve; appraisal results are reviewed with the employee.
- Appraisals that are disputed can be appealed to a higher level for review.
- The organization's policy provides for frequent performance review.

Above all, the appraisal system should not discriminate against any group or have an adverse effect on them in employment opportunities. As a rough rule of thumb, a selection rate for any legally protected group that is less than 80 percent of the rate for the group with the highest rate of selection comprises an adverse impact. (This is also known as the ''four-fifths rule.'') In general, if no adverse impact in the selection process is demonstrated with regard to the 80 percent rule, demonstration of each component's validity will not be required. Even where there is an absence of adverse impact at the bottom line, appraisal procedures that are so subjective by their very nature invite scrutiny and may be struck down.

It is not up to the decentralized line and staff manager to monitor the company's selection, training, promotion, and performance appraisal procedures to assure compliance with the four-fifths rule. But, again, employees are assigned to work for managers, and the latter hold jobs at strategic junctures whereby personnel decisions can be made to implement equal employment opportunity.

The HR/PMD should monitor all human-resource planning and development so that it is in compliance with the law. The manager carries out daily administrative actions, providing factual data so that compliance reports will contain the necessary factual information to display the existence of equal employment opportunity.

In a broader sense, all the guidelines we have set forth suggest not only how to install lawful procedures but also how to implement sound systems that are desirable for effective human-resource management even if they were not legally mandated.

The human-resource management task in the last two decades of the twentieth century will be a formidable one and will take place in an increasingly litigious atmosphere, until equal employment opportunity has become the way of life in American business and the public sector.

In the future we may see an open society with the free and unfettered mobility of people based upon their talents. Performance appraisal could be designed and administered in such a way to help America move toward such a society—one that would protect human dignity and pride and stamp out prejudice.

45

If the name of the game is vitality, goal attainment, corporate or agency leadership, or the provision of high-quality products or services, then an adequate MBO-based performance appraisal system linked to the administration of rewards is indispensable!

In closing, we come full circle to our starting point. The chapter title above says it all. This book should have shown how performance appraisal can be instrumental to successful management by practicing managers.

How can a manager soar like an eagle if he works with turkey systems? He needs to fly and acquire the means to get off the ground. An MBO-based performance appraisal system linked to the administration of rewards will allow him to take off!

APPENDIX A

Excerpts from Prevailing Federal Legislation pertaining to Equal Opportunity in Employment

---

THE EQUAL PAY AMENDMENTS to the Fair Labor Standards Act of 1938 and Title VII of the Civil Rights Act of 1964 allow differences in pay based upon "merit," which is what we mean by "performance" in this book. Relevant quotations from the two laws are provided below for the reader's convenience.

Legal Background

The broadest concept of equal pay for equal work is embodied in 43 U.S.C. ¶ 2000e-2 of Title VII of the Civil Rights Act of 1964, as amended. Accordingly, it is an unlawful employment practice for an employer:

—To fail or refuse to hire or to discharge any individual, or otherwise to discriminate against any individual with respect to his compensation, terms, conditions, or privileges of employment, because of such individual's race, color, religion, sex, or national origin; or

—To limit, segregate, or classify his employees or applicants for employment in any way which would deprive or tend to deprive any individual of employment opportunities or otherwise adversely affect his status as an employee because of such individual's race, color, religion, sex, or national origin.

A narrower concept of equal pay is found in 29 U.S.C. ¶ 206(d)(1) of the Equal Pay Act of 1963, which is an amendment to the Fair Labor Standards Act of 1938:

> No employer having employees subject to any provisions of this section shall discriminate, within any establishment in which such employees are employed, between employees on the basis of sex by paying wages to employees in such establishment at a rate less than the rate at which he pays wages to employees of the opposite sex in such establishment for work on jobs the performance of which requires equal skill, effort, and responsibility, and which are performed under similar working conditions, except where such payment is made pursuant to (i) a seniority system; (ii) a merit system; (iii) a system which measures earnings by quantity or quality of production; or (iv) a differential based on any other factor other than sex: provided, that an employer who is paying a wage rate differential in violation of this subsection shall not, in order to comply with the provisions of this subsection, reduce the wage rate of any employee.

The Equal Pay Act has wide application and applies to firms that have two or more employees. It is broader than the applicability of Title VII, but for all practical purposes both laws importantly affect all employees in the United States. Through Title IX of the Education Amendments Act of 1972, coverage of the equal pay provisions was extended to executive, administrative, professional, and outside sales personnel.

The legislative history of the Civil Rights Act of 1964 provides only general guidance as to what may be lawful in respect to performance appraisal and leaves it up to the HR/PMD, manager, and citizen to figure out how and when the law is violated.

A study of case law would provide more specific guidance but the significance of case judgments is best analyzed by an attorney who specializes in personnel and labor-relations law. Therefore, readers who require an understanding of the legal issues involved in specific situations in their companies and agencies should obviously consult an attorney.

APPENDIX B

Hamilton Jordan's Homemade Performance Appraisal System (Graphic Rating Scale) Applied to the Presidency of Jimmy Carter.

If Jimmy Took Ham's Test

A remarkable form designed to assess the strengths and weaknesses of high Administration officials was distributed last week by new Chief of Staff Hamilton Jordan. It was devised by Michael Berman, staff counsel and deputy chief of staff to Vice President Walter Mondale, and Len Hirsch,

an outside consultant to Jordan. Several management experts who studied the form declared that it told more about the raters than it did about the rated. They viewed it variously as "unsophisticated," "unprofessional," "unfair" and "unreliable." The hastily devised form even included two spelling errors, "savy" and "uncomfortable." Here is a specimen on which Washington Bureau Chief Robert Ajemian has evaluated the country's most important employee.

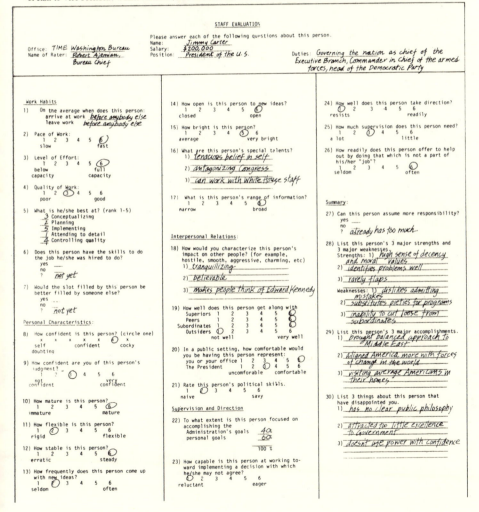

Source: Time 114, no. 5 (July 30, 1979): 19. Reprinted with permission from the Time-Life Publishing Company, New York, New York.

NOTES

1. Performance appraisal has had more euphemistic aliases than almost any other topic in human-resource management. Two of the earliest terms for it were "merit rating" and "efficiency rating," both suggesting the idea that employees were to be "rated" for the goodness (perhaps quality and quantity) of their production—how efficient they were in a certain sense. In time the word "performance" supplanted "merit" and "efficiency" and rating gave way to appraisal, evaluation, or review, all of which are virtually synonymous unless we wish to make a distinction between "evaluation" as attempted objective measurement and "appraisal" as a loose mixture of objective and subjective attempts to estimate how well an employee performs in a stipulated period. All of this, of course, begs the definition of performance. Performance is composed of ends and means: the perceived results that an employee turns out on the job as well as the behavior he displays to attain those results.

2. Contemporary authors try to avoid sexism by using "he or she" rather than "he" whenever possible in order to include both males and females. Four females share my domicile and they do not consider me sexist. I hope the reader does not consider me sexist because I use the generic "he" and "his" unabashedly throughout this book to avoid redundancy and awkwardness.

3. See Appendix A for an excerpt from prevailing federal legislation pertaining to equal opportunity in employment.

4. The best single source of original materials on rating systems of the past—the antique gallery of the field—such as forced choice, critical incidents, man-to-man rating, and field review, is Thomas L. Whistler and Shirley F. Harper, eds., *Performance Appraisal: Research and Practice* (New York: Holt, Rinehart and Winston, 1962). A shorter review of old systems can be found in Thomas H. Patten, Jr., *Pay: Employee Compensation and Incentive Plans* (New York: Free Press, 1977), pp. 352–357.

5. BARS are discussed in Chapter 38.

6. A national tempest in a teapot during President Carter's administration swirled around a graphic rating scale that was poorly conceived

and unhappily received by cabinet members who were asked to administer them. See Appendix B.

7. There is nothing wrong with any type of appraisal format that is conceptually similar to what we are advocating. The form we are discusing is a prototype presented only for the reader's consideration.

8. The word "game" is used here in the sense made popular by Eric Berne, *Games People Play* (New York: Ballantine Books, 1964), and Thomas Harris, *I'm OK—Your're OK: A Practical Guide to Transactional Analysis* (New York: Harper and Row, 1967).

9. Included among the best books on interviewing would be Richard Fear, *The Evaluation Interview* (New York: McGraw-Hill, 1958), rev. ed., pp. 102-154, 215-258; Felix M. Lopez, Jr., *Personnel Interviewing: Theory and Practice* (New York: McGraw-Hill, 1965) pp. 3-65, 125-209; and Robert L. Kahn and Charles F. Cannell, *The Dynamics of Interviewing: Theory, Technique, and Cases* (New York: Wiley, 1957), pp. 3-252.

10. The best discussion of the details of standard setting and techniques in MBO is in George S. Odiorne, *MBO II: A System of Managerial Leadership* (Belmont, Calif.: Fearon Pitman, 1979), pp. 127-175. For the application of MBO to hourly employees, see R. Henry Migliore, *MBO: Blue Collar to Executive* (Washington, D.C.: Bureau of National Affairs, 1977).

11. Again, Odiorne's work should be consulted. See ibid., pp. 235-257.

12. For some reason, it is often not remembered that Drucker, commonly regarded as the founder of MBO almost three decades ago, formulated the concept as "management by objectives and self-control," clearly stating the idea of a disciplined approach to managerial work. See Peter F. Drucker. *The Practice of Management* (New York: Harper, 1954), pp. 121-136.

13. For the details of design that apply here, see Patten, *Pay: Employee Compensation and Incentive Plans*, pp. 572-586.

14. Ibid.

BIBLIOGRAPHY

THE FOLLOWING BOOKS should be useful in getting a handle on the subject. Periodical literature on performance review is so extensive and repetitious that I have omitted reference to it entirely but I recommend it to readers who wish to pursue in-depth treatments of specific facets of the subject.

CUMMINGS, LARRY L. and SCHWAB, DONALD P. *Performance in Organizations: Determinants and Appraisal.* Glenview: Scott, Foresman, 1973. 176 pp.

DRUCKER, PETER F. *The Practice of Management.* New York: Harper and Row, 1954. 404 pp.

FEAR, RICHARD A. *The Evaluation Interview.* Rev. ed. New York: McGraw-Hill, 1958. 288 pp.

HENDERSON, RICHARD. *Performance Appraisal: Theory to Practice.* Reston: Va.: Reston Publishing Co., 1980. 310 pp.

KAHN, ROBERT L. and CANNELL, CHARLES F. *The Dynamics of Interviewing: Theory, Technique, and Cases.* New York: Wiley, 1957. 252 pp.

KELLOGG, MARION S. *What to Do about Performance Appraisal.* Rev. ed. New York: American Management Associations, 1975. 209 pp.

KOONTZ, HAROLD. *Appraising Managers as Managers.* New York: McGraw-Hill, 1971. 239 pp.

LAMBERT, CLARK. *Field Sales Performance Appraisal.* New York: Wiley, 1979. 313 pp.

LATHAM, GARY P. and WEXLEY, KENNETH N. *Increasing Productivity through Performance Appraisal.* Reading, Mass.: Addison-Wesley Publishing Co., 1980. 262 pp.

LEFTON, ROBERT E. et al. *Effective Motivation through Performance Appraisal.* New York: Wiley, 1977. 348 pp.

LOPEZ, FELIX M. *Evaluating Employee Performance.* Chicago: Public Personnel Association, 1968. 306 pp.

MIGLIORE, R. HENRY. *MBO: Blue Collar to Top Executive.* Rockville, Md.: Bureau of National Affairs, 1977. 192 pp.

ODIORNE, GEORGE S. *MBO II: A System of Managerial Leadership for the 80's.* Belmont, Calif.: Fearon-Pitman, 1979. 360 pp.

PATTEN, THOMAS H., JR. *Manpower Planning and the Development of Human Resources.* New York: Wiley, 1971. 737 pp.

————. *Organizational Development through Team-building.* New York: Wiley, 1981. 295 pp.

————. *Pay: Employee Compensation and Incentive Plans.* New York: Free Press, 1977. 607 pp.

WHISTLER, THOMAS L. and HARPER, SHIRLEY F., eds. *Performance Appraisal: Research and Practice.* New York: Holt, Rinehart, and Winston, 1962. 593 pp.

WINSTANLEY, NATHAN B., ed. *Current Readings in Performance Appraisal.* Pittsburgh: American Compensation Association, 1974. 251 pp.

INDEX

INDEX